Stewards of History

A Study of the Nature of a Moral Deed

by

Caryl Johnston

"Woe to the race that does not stop at the crossroads before continuing on its way, which does not make a problem out of its own inner life, which does not feel the heroic necessity of justifying its destiny and of throwing light on its mission in history!"

Ortega y Gasset, *Meditations on Quixote*

RoseDog Books
PITTSBURGH, PENNSYLVANIA 15222

The contents of this work including, but not limited to, the accuracy of events, people, and places depicted; opinions expressed; permission to use previously published materials included; and any advice given or actions advocated are solely the responsibility of the author, who assumes all liability for said work and indemnifies the publisher against any claims stemming from publication of the work.

The Thoroughbred Colt: Identity and Moral Will in a Southern Family, 1999.

All Rights Reserved
Copyright © 2011 by Caryl Johnston

No part of this book may be reproduced or transmitted, downloaded, distributed, reverse engineered, or stored in or introduced into any information storage and retrieval system, in any form or by any means, including photocopying and recording, whether electronic or mechanical, now known or hereinafter invented without permission in writing from the publisher.

RoseDog Books
701 Smithfield Street
Pittsburgh, PA 15222
Visit our website at *www.rosedogbookstore.com*

ISBN:978-1-4349-8473-9
eISBN:978-1-4349-7466-2

John Hartwell Cocke on his favorite horse, Roebuck.
Painting by Edward Troye; original in the White House.
Courtesy of the White House Historical Association

Acknowledgements

Many have encouraged and assisted with this book. I appreciate the assistance of my brother Paul C. Johnston and my cousin, Joseph F. Johnston, Jr. I wish to thank John Lukacs, Eugene Genovese, Robert S. Horner and Robert R. Horner, Jr. for reading and commenting on the manuscript.

I wish to thank Michael F. Plunkett, Curator, Christina Deane, and the staff of the Special Collections, University of Virginia Library, for assistance with the Cocke Papers. My thanks and appreciation to the late Anne Freudenberg; also Vesta Gordon, Doug and Catherine Wheeler, Dudley Cocke, Boyd Coyner, Marvin Whiting, Jim Baggett, Raymond and the late Frances Orf, and my late uncle and aunt, Joe and Betty Johnston.

I would also like to thank recent readers Alphonse Vinh, Sam Frederick, and Martin Croes. I wish to thank Ron Petrou in particular, for his appreciation and enthusiasm for the work, and for giving me the steady encouragement to publish it.

Contents

Preface ix
Prologue: Western Interior..xi
I. Miss Clara 1
II. The Old General 7
III. The Blooded Colt..22
IV. Soldier of the Cross 33
    i. Law of Generations..33
    ii. Work of Regeneration..35
    iii. An Awakened Act of Neglect..43
V. Fruit of the Vine 48
VI. A Covenant, Not a Right 55
VII. The Magic City..64
VIII. The Other Side of Something Remembered 79
    i. Tribal Loyalty 79
    ii. Vulcan...82
IX. Promise of Generations 92
X. The Living Being..102
Epilogue: Intimacy of Fact 109
Postscript to "Stewards of History" 111
Appendix One: A Note on Thomas Jefferson 116
Appendix Two: "But... this was not death, but life..." 121
Bibliography 123

Preface

An author who produces a second edition of a work which never achieved a proper first edition must be either very audacious or very persistent. The one advantage of Internet publishing — and there are not many advantages — is that the book cries out for revision. It testifies to the unfinished and the incomplete.

For certain kinds of books this would not be the right message. But for *The Thoroughbred Colt* — now renamed *Stewards of History* — it is the essence of its spirit. It is a book about history, and history is never finished or complete; it is never something over and done with. History, too, cries out for revision, rewriting, reliving, rethinking.

A couple of years ago I attended the Southern Women's Historical Association meeting, where I heard Jacqueline Dowd Hall characterize history-writing as "the sympathetic reconstruction of an absent past." I remember thinking at the time how different this was from the way I felt about *The Thoroughbred Colt*. This book is a passionate engagement with a past that is all too present, an inescapable past. How can people think the past is either absent or dead? It's taken me years (most of my adult life, in fact) to deal with the present-past. I feel I have only recently arrived in the present-present. And I'm still not there yet. There's always yesterday.

I'm grateful to the people who expressed enthusiasm for the Buy Books on the Web version of *The Thoroughbred Colt* despite its many flaws and underwhelming appearance. My brother Paul gave me a great compliment, concerning a philosopher we both admire. "Ortega [y Gasset] would have liked it." I have incorporated Ortega's motto from the *Meditations on Quixote* because I think it expresses this book's deepest purpose.

Randall Miller, a professor of history at St. Joseph's University in Philadelphia, wrote me on October 10, 1999: "… I read with awe and admiration your *stunning* book, *The Thoroughbred Colt,* which contains biography, memoir & even novel in a way that Faulkner would appreciate... With a novelist's eye & the sure hand of a skilled historian, you have given us . . . a way of seeing the past through many lenses. Please, please let the world know of your work . . . I am adding it to my students' reading list . . . "

Randall Miller's book, *Dear Master: Letters of a Slave Family*, is an important source for the life of John Hartwell Cocke. Dr. Miller was delighted to find that someone was continuing to tell Cocke's story. "To the casual student of black slavery in America," his book began, "it might seem wrongheaded and mean to begin a black family chronicle with a paean of praise to a white slave owner." Indeed. I am happy to report that since *The Thoroughbred Colt* appeared in its Internet edition, I learned that John Hartwell Cocke was honored in 1996 during Black History Month in Norfolk, Virginia. Nearly a hundred and fifty years after the fall of slavery, this is a touching reminder of the staying power of honorable remembrance.

Dr. Miller was generous to speak of the "sure hand of a skilled historian" — an estimation I would certainly not claim for myself. I do think, though, that how a story crystallizes out of its material is a mysterious process all its own. The difference between history and fiction is not only that the former "really happened" and the latter is imagined to have happened. There is a deeper, more unearthly difference between fact and fiction. The writer of history has a real relationship to the dead. The dead in history are real, and I believe they suffer if the stories we tell of them are false or shallow. But how are we, the living, to know the stories of the dead? We can only hope that the moment of quickening will come to us in our journey from research to inspiration – when we may hear the stories of the dead, and know of their passion and fact.

Birmingham, February 20, 2002

Prologue: Western Interior

In American history, the historian James Truslow Adams wrote, there was always the frontier, "a state of mind and a golden opportunity." But in 1890, he said, all this changed. The Census Report of that year announced the closing of the frontier. "For a century and a half," Adams writes, "we had been occupied in conquering and exploiting a continent, and by 1890 the task was completed. It had been an adventure of youth. Now it was over."[1]

A century later, a very different West has come to occupy the attention of the restless multitudes — at least the intellectually restless ones. But this West is not an adventure of youth nor an undiscovered frontier. This is the West of our cultural inheritance, the legacy of the classical world and of European Christendom. In the early 1990's Yale University twice refused considerable donations to support programs in Western studies, "a further sign of faculty and administration hostility to Western culture," one student said.[2]

To Glenn Tinder, the revolt against the Western heritage is a symptom of the "crisis of knowledge and authority" that we are living through: the problem of *foundations*. "… How is it that so many thinkers, both in this country and elsewhere, have failed so signally to deal with this crisis? … What explains the fact that after more than twenty-five centuries of philosophy and nearly twenty centuries of Christianity we find our lives — at least our intellectual lives — running along the very brink of nihilism?"[3]

---

[1] James Truslow Adams, *The Epic of America*, New York, 1931, p. 306. Adams is indirectly paying homage to Frederick Jackson Turner's thesis concerning "The Significance of the Frontier in American History," first delivered as an address in 1893, in which, according to *Chambers Biographical Dictionary,* Turner "boldly assert[ed] that American democracy derived from its frontier experience and not from its European inheritance."

[2] *The Washington Times* , Sept. 19-24, 1995.

[3] Glenn Tinder, "At the End of Pragmatism," *First Things,* October, 1995.

It is a good question — sharp and eloquent— and I want to take it as a general starting point for this book, which is a search for foundations through the medium of historical consciousness.

I am a Southerner. It is often said that the South has managed to preserve a unique sense of historical consciousness, though there is wide disagreement regarding its scope and nature. Eugene Genovese, in his book *The Southern Conservative Tradition: Achievements and Limitations of an American Conservatism,* says that even "those who despise the southern tradition have inadvertently conceded its historical preponderance." It is, at any rate, a tradition that has much to do with literature.

I note, first of all, that the literature of remembrance is a prominent feature of Southern writing in, and just before, my time. The collapse of society following the Civil War and Reconstruction must have been a painful reality for those fleeing from what C. Vann Woodward called *The Burden of Southern History.* Certainly a sense of loss figured to a great extent in this burden. Thomas Wolfe said that *You Can't Go Home Again;* James Agee wrote about it in *A Death in the Family.* Paul Hemphill, a compatriot of mine, took Wolfe seriously in his *Leaving Birmingham.* He took a long look — but still, he left.

Many Southerners, black and white, joined Willie Morris in the migration *North Toward Home.*[4] Or those who stayed remained, like Virginia Durr, *Outside the Magic Circle*, reading, with Walker Percy, the *Signposts in a Strange Land.* But there were those, like Walker Percy's great-uncle, who learned that "If you die it is natural; if you live you have learned pity and the strength of silence."[5] What "piety begot upon imagination"[6] was that there was spiritual gain to be wrested from loss, oppression, and alienation. V.S. Naipaul even found something morally triumphant in the black culture of the segregated South. A kind of death of the soul came in with integration, one black Southerner put it — "It was a kind of death that had come to black people in some ways with desegregation and the consequent loss of community."[7]

"Community": this was known to both the white and black Southerner. The smallest community of all, in my day, was that of liberal Southerners who had joined, in Birmingham and elsewhere, the cause for racial equality. But even liberal Southerners could sound at times like the Agrarians — those thinkers and literary men who gathered in Nashville, Tennessee, in the 1930's and mounted, in their book *I'll Take My Stand,* a fierce polemic against modernism. Modernism is individualistic, not community oriented; it wants to break away from regionalism, rootedness, remembrance. Before it became the cult of contemporaneity it was the creed of economic self-interest: "And I re-

---

[4] An interesting reversal of this trend — Diane McWhorter's recent *Carry Me Home,* a massive compendium of information about Birmingham in the civil rights era.

[5] William Alexander Percy, *Lanterns on the Levee*, New York, Knopf, 1941, p. 79.

[6] James Branch Cabell, *Let Me Lie*, New York, 1947, p. 92.

[7] V.S. Naipaul, *A Turn in the South*, New York, Knopf, 1989, p. 67.

membered that while Southerners had talked for fifty years of a past full of heroes, of a world in which tragedy was a noble neighbor, men from New York and Boston had devoted themselves quietly to the fixing of freight rates," writes Jonathan Daniels, in *A Southerner Discovers the South*.

The Agrarians objected to the idea of economic self-interest as the goal of life. Even the egalitarian racial sentiments of a liberal Southerner like Virginia Durr do not prevent her from echoing the Southern Agrarian critique of "economism:"

> "The South was and still is, in my opinion, a colony of the North. After we were defeated in the Civil War, they bought us up for a nickel on the dollar, and they still own us. When I lived in Birmingham, it was a company town, just completely owned by Northern corporations. The owners would come down in their private railroad cars. It was like being visited by a king."[8]

She goes on to say that when she was growing up "everybody was preaching industrialization" — people like Henry W. Grady in Atlanta and Booker T. Washington in Tuskegee. The idea was "Northern money, industrialize, and bring in the money."

To some, even worse than economic self-interest was the "pernicious moralism and venality" which lay behind Northern liberalism's war against the South. In 1984 I received a letter from a friend in Springfield, Massachusetts; maybe he thought I was ready by then for a bit of 'revisionist' history. He said he was reading a book about the Confederacy that "smashes all the stereotypes about the Civil War and . . . reveals the truth about the Confederacy in its purely American hopes." He goes on to say:

> "The northern liberals manipulated the South into an impossible position solely to destroy a way of life that was Christian and honorable, using slavery as 'the big lie' by which northern liberalism's true aims (consolidated political power and economic control) could be achieved... In short, the North was hypocritical and venal, jealous of the South's independent 'American' attitude...the defeat of the South was the defeat of the American ideal; and after all, you and I live in an historical period only 120 years removed from that betrayal."[9]

"The South is, or ought to be, of compelling interest to that thoughtful minority concerned with conserving what is left of Christianity and Western

---

[8] Virginia Durr, *Outside the Magic Circle*, 1985, p. 33. This particular passage has a personal resonance for me. Sometime in the early 1950's my father took us children down to the train station, where we met a gentleman in the luxury of his own private railroad car. I don't remember who he was, but I remember feeling very impressed with his comfortable accommodations.

[9] Letter, Samuel Cuthbert to Caryl Johnston, January 20, 1984.

civilization," wrote Clyde Wilson, in *Why the South Will Survive*. And this book — a commemoration of the fiftieth anniversary of *I'll Take My Stand*, says something about why the South *should* survive — as Clyde Wilson puts it in his introduction — but also about the particular difficulties involved. Andrew Lytle remarked in his Afterword: "I can wish now that *I'll Take My Stand* and the writings that followed it had made it clearer that, in defending what was left of Southern life, we were defending our common European inheritance... To put it in religious terms, we have lost the covenant with God..."[10]

Here Andrew Lytle, one of the original contributors, identifies the chief shortcoming of Southern conservatism: which, to Richard Weaver, consisted in the South's failure to enunciate a "metaphysic of position." What was the "Agrarian Defense" or, for that matter, the significance of the Old South? To Richard Weaver in *The Southern Tradition at Bay*, its significance lay in the fact that the South was *"the last non-materialist civilization in the Western World."* Yet Southerners did not build on this foundation a coherent metaphysics. The Southern tradition was one which, according to Weaver, "the South ... has imperfectly understood and little used." At best, he concludes –

> "Looking at the whole of the South's promise and achievement, I would be unwilling to say it offers a foundation, or, because of the accidents of history, even an example. The most that it offers is a challenge. And the challenge is to save the human spirit by re-creating a non-materialist society. Only this can rescue us from a future of nihilism, urged on by the demoniacal force of technology and by our own moral defeatism."

* * *

In an American history course in college, I learned that one historian (whose name I do not recall) defined the two poles of American spirituality to be Puritanism and Transcendentalism.

I remember, in high school, reading a patch of text from Jonathan Edwards' sermon, "Sinners in the Hands of an Angry God." It was unbelievably vivid; in fact it is the only thing I remember reading from the tenth grade, the selection anthologized in one of those Norton textbooks for young people. Who can forget the image of the spider dangled over the eternal flames? I never could, and I am sure that the parishioners of that worthy Puritan divine who heard this sermon could never forget it too.

Maybe Emerson, the representative Transcendentalist, remembered it too well, and was fleeing from the sense of sin. His "Oversoul" is very different from the holy soul, or even the historical soul. Emerson resigned his Unitarian ministry in 1832 over the issue of the Lord's Supper: "This mode of com-

---

[10] Andrew Lytle, "Afterword *A Semi-Centennial* in *Why the South Will Survive*, Univ Georgia, 1981, p. 225.

memorating Christ is not suitable to me," he said. One wonders: what other mode was there?

In neither of the two poles of American spirituality mentioned by that history professor was there any mention of a specifically *Southern* contribution to American spirituality. I believe that we have a need for it, and this book may be considered an attempt to rectify that omission.

An ancestor of mine, John Hartwell Cocke of Virginia, was a younger contemporary of Thomas Jefferson, and held in esteem by him. The two cooperated on a number of projects — most notably in the founding of the University of Virginia.

The friendship between these two men was genuine, as were their religious differences. One day, before I had the idea of writing this book, I imagined that Mr. Jefferson and Mr. Cocke had a conversation about religion. As it turned out, the "conversation" I actually imagined was not quite that — it was more of an interior monologue — but that it *could have happened* became the occasion for examining General Cocke's life, his two marriages, his ideas about religion and slave emancipation. Cocke's way in slave emancipation was, as the poet Robert Frost said, "the road not taken." Cocke's Christian convictions inspired him to develop a practical response for dealing with the problem of slavery. Yet his was virtually a "lost Christianity."

I say a "lost Christianity" — because there were many Christians who supported, or at least justified, the slavery cause. Eugene Genovese has written with insight and compassion about many of these individuals, whose arguments, he believes, made hash of the work of the abolitionists. He writes that in the views promoted by Southern Christians, "... the defense of slavery emerged as only a strain in a much broader defense of Christendom." It was an "authentic worldview," he says, which "integrated Christian morals, political principles, and cultural standards." [11] Still, he acknowledges, it was a tragedy of a "strong, honorable, gifted people who ended by placing their formidable talents in the service of an enormity."

General Cocke never placed his talents in the service of such an "enormity." He stands out in his single-minded dedication to train and prepare "his people" for freedom, and never (except at the end, when the war was lost) did he seek to justify servitude. His indeed was "the road not taken."

General Cocke left many written remembrances of himself — letters, journals, papers — now preserved at the University of Virginia Library. The Cocke Family Papers form one of the largest repositories of nineteenth-century family history in America, and I have been able to draw on only a small portion of this material. But more than archives, there is Bremo — the mansion built by General Cocke in Virginia, which I visited as a child, where I was married, and which, time permitting, I still visit occasionally. The living record of the past was in this architecture of family memory.

---

[11] Eugene Genovese, *The Southern Front*, Missouri, 1995, p. 106.

It is not difficult to imagine General Cocke being there — at Bremo — setting out for Charlottesville on his horse early one May morning, trotting beside fields with rising mists, seeing the first of the field swallows. He tells us so himself, when he went to visit Mr. Jefferson at Monticello.

Narrative is, above all, a *relation*, and it is no accident that "relation" encompasses the idea of "kinship" as well as "giving an account of." Telling the story is to affirm the *relation*. I am the occasionally autobiographical narrator, not because I am in pursuit of myself, but because I am in pursuit of knowledge as *relation*. And this *integration* or *relation* refers not only to the effort to integrate the life of my ancestor and relatives into my own life, not only to the shaping of an ongoing Christian understanding of history, but also to the task of telling a "metaphysics of place."

What is the relationship between events and thoughts, between the mind and the world, between the stories we tell and the people we are? These are the questions that Glenn Tinder meant by "foundations." They have become important now, not just for politics but for life. It is in search of the foundational stories that this book is dedicated — to the enduring stories that renew our covenant with the generations.

"Miss Clara," 1901.

She was born on the longest day of the year,
    during the Reconstruction era, in a region of rivers,
Fluvanna County, Virginia. In 1905 she married
and went to live in Alabama.
She had three children, two sons and a daughter,
and the second of her sons
    was my father.

I. Miss Clara

It always seemed right that she was born on the longest day of the year, June 21, in 1880. For she lived to be nearly a hundred. In the early part of her life, where I am concerned, she belongs to the *researched* past. In her later years she is a figure of my *remembered* past.

She grew up in surroundings of singular beauty, at Lower Bremo, in Fluvanna County, Virginia. This house began as a hunting lodge on grounds deeded to Cocke ancestors by the King of England in 1725. The hunting lodge was later remodeled as a country house in Queen Anne style, and possessed a beautiful flower garden in back and a sweeping view of the James River low grounds in front.

Clara Cocke was the great-granddaughter of General John Hartwell Cocke, about which more in due course. To the west of Lower Bremo, about two miles up the river, stood the mansion Bremo designed by General Cocke. My grandmother often said how, in her youth, she would ride her horse up this river road and see Bremo in the distance. At that time Bremo was owned by another branch of the family. "I knew I wanted to buy it back," she said.

It was the Reconstruction era and Clara's mother, a widow, was not rich. Still, Clara came of age in what must have been, for a person in her situation, a peaceful time. She acknowledges as much in an entry from her journal, dated January 1, 1901. Her carefree pursuits are at odds with her historical consciousness:

> "Ah, what idle things I write down here! Nothing historic, nothing that could be of the slightest interest to future generations — not even a touching love story. Really unkind of me, I think."

There were things to learn, like the arts of society:

> "... The 'graciousness' that Mother is always talking about is indeed a great thing. I am always making up my mind to practice or acquire it, but I am afraid I often forget... I have always had a half-acknowledged worship of the *dames* of the French salon with all their grace and charm. The charm was a simple matter after all, according to Madame Récamier, who said she kept hers by the use of two words — [whenever] anyone came, she said *'enfin!'* when they left, *'déjà?'* "

She describes in some detail her thoughts on social life, one important aspect of which was going to balls:

> "... Whatever it is, there are no good times like the ones there [at the University of Virginia] and I have been to balls in Charleston, germans in Richmond & cotillions in New York — but there is nothing like the University. Surely Thomas Jefferson built these arcades for Easter girls to stroll beneath on moon-lit and star-lit nights, and arranged 'the Lawn' and the stately old Rotunda with a view to fostering sentiment as well as cold knowledge...

> "And then, there is an especial 'special attraction' who may come strolling down the arcades or crossing the walks at any moment, it's all the more thrilling and exciting. We got to the University two or three days before Easter, and from that time on we were in a whirl. There was not a moment of the day (or night) that the doorbell or the telephone bell was not ringing or that we were not going somewhere or having something exciting happen.

>> "We both [Clara and her sister Virginia] certainly had great 'rushes' and had more men than we knew what to do with... Almost everyone considered Virginia the beauty of Easter and she did look lovely — especially one night when she wore her green *crêpe de chine* gown and carried a huge bunch of American beauties..."

The ambition to buy back the Bremo estate was fulfilled in 1926 when Clara, by now the wife of Forney Johnston, found herself in means to do so. Clara and her future husband courted when he was a law student at the University of Virginia — perhaps he was one of her 'rushes.' Their marriage was celebrated at Bremo in 1905.

The son of the governor of Alabama, Forney began a successful law practice in Birmingham. After their wedding the couple moved to this raw steel town, not yet fifty years old, that "had a saloon on every corner," as Clara once put it.

Bremo in the days before Forney and Clara purchased it was owned by some elderly cousins, who, finding the rooms and attics of the old house crammed with old letters, threw them all out. They saved only the signatures — from James Madison, James Monroe, Thomas Jefferson. Few events are so revealing of the change in historical consciousness, as this. The distance between ourselves and the Founding Fathers is collapsed, as it were, by the presence of those letters. But we come near to the Founders only to be turned away again; their presence becomes an absence. Into this absence enters the touchingly naive concept of monetary, because historical, value — as evidenced by the saving of the signatures.

My grandparents lived in Birmingham but went to Bremo every summer where, by my time, they were engaged in all manner of renovations and farming. My earliest memories of visits there in the summer are patriarchal, matriarchal, familial. The patriarch, Grandpa, was involved with the installation of bathrooms, alignment of flagstones and pointing of bricks. His hours-long visits to the hardware store in Charlottesville bespoke a certain relief from the practice of law, his pleasure in fixing, tinkering, handyman's work. It bespoke too of the grinding patience of his daughter-in-law and grandchildren waiting in a hot car in the sizzling Charlottesville summer for him — interminable, methodical, punctilious to the last bag of thumbtacks — to emerge.

To be sure, the bathrooms were an improvement over outhouses. But there was still the wood stove in the kitchen and Lucy who prepared batter cakes with the tops charred and smelling of wood smoke. There was an electric stove in the kitchen but she never used it as much. There was Ervin too, who worked for my grandparents in Birmingham but drove the car up for them in the summers, and did the butlering and chauffeuring. I used to go and watch him in the yard behind the garage, where he would catch a scrabbling chicken running about there, wring its neck, and pluck its feathers off for dinner.

There was also a white caretaking staff, and it was the daughter of one of these who attended to the milk cow in those days. I used to accompany Anna Dove, the stout and pock-marked milkmaid (hardly the rosy-cheeked English milkmaid, but as good a dew-dabbler in the morning as any one of these) as she would shuffle down to the barn, pail in hand. Along with barn cats I would taste the milk that reeked, in the early summers, of wild onion. Later Lucy would churn some of that milk into butter and pat the yellow lumps into little balls.

We always dressed for dinner.[12] As our visits often coincided with visits of other relatives, dinners for ten or twelve were not unusual. Then there were second and third cousins down at Lower Bremo, a more exotic clan of Cockes who hailed from Mississippi or Washington, D.C. or Argentina. It was mostly during the decade of the 1950's that these nineteenth-century summers were passed. At the time I suppose I never gave it much thought but accepted these experiences as part of the order of things.

---

[12] "Not quite— dressing for dinner to a Virginian means black tie." Editorial note from Joseph F. Johnston, Jr.

In the library at Bremo were the remnants of General Cocke's gentleman's collection, mostly polite literature, history and books of agricultural import.[13] Upstairs, under the attic (moved later, no doubt, by members of a less pious generation) were the Bibles, sermons, and evangelical tracts from another century — the leaves brown, faded, watermarked, survivors from the Age of Faith. General Cocke's presence was strongly felt at Bremo, though upon occasion one or another member of the older generation — parents, uncles or aunts, would speak mirthfully of Cocke's temperance crusade or of his puritanical inclinations.

Still, the Old General was there, a benign yet sobering presence, from the chair he used in the library, from Edward Troye's portrait of him astride his favorite horse, Roebuck. The original of this portrait is in the White House; my grandparents had a copy of it over the mantelpiece. Erect on his black horse, with his sword pointing upward, and in uniform with sash and epaulets, the Old General is — despite the sobriquet — beardless and young. He cuts a gallant figure, but his dark eyes, accentuated by the fullness and length of the black eyebrows, suggest preoccupations other than gallantry. The landscape behind him looks more like Tuscany than Virginia: had he been garbed in a monk's habit, the Old General might have looked like Savanarola.

---

[13] "Nowhere else in America could one find such splendid libraries as once existed in Old Virginia. Amongst the great libraries were those collected by Washington, Jefferson, Madison, the Skipwiths of Prestwould, Randolph of Roanoke, Saint George Tucker, Littleton Tazewell, John Hartwell Cocke, and Hugh Grigsby. In the case of the Virginia gentleman, his home was not his castle, but his library." Alphonse Vinh, "What Made the Virginia Tradition?" Typescript, n.d.

Invocation

I stood listening in the wood
Near the stone basin of the spring.
It was clotted with leaves;
The spring had ceased to flow.
I was listening for you, or being listened to,
And I will not say, "This is the story
You told me to tell," or "Here
Is what I heard you say."
We are bound by honor and by blood
And by memory more than either.
These three figures emerge to hold me
To your silence in an act of faith.
I cleared the leaves away from the spring —
Sadly, I could not drink from there again.
But the stillness gives me leave to speak.

Bremo: three views

II. The Old General:
John Hartwell Cocke, 1780-1866

General Cocke set a high moral tone to his pursuits. With the placement of the cornerstone at Bremo on July 8, 1818, Cocke wrote in his diary that his first thought had been to consecrate the new residence to the memory of his wife. But, on further thought, he makes a dedicatory vow both more comprehensive and less personal:

> *May the all wise disposer of events, in Whose omniscient foresight it hath seemed good to forbid its dedication to her whom I perhaps too much idolized, convert it into a temple wherein I may sacrifice all vain and worldly affections and prepare myself by penitency, humility and devotion, an offering fit for the acceptance of the Eternal. And since it has pleased Almighty God to continue this estate in the possession of my forefathers from the first occupancy of this country by a civilized and Christian people, I beseech Him that it may be handed down to my latest posterity so long as they follow the example which I pray Him to assist me in setting . . . of hospitality without ostentation; justice and humanity towards all men, especially that unfortunate race of dependents who . . . are too often victims of cruelty and misrule; a generous consideration of those to whom worldly goods have been less liberally dispensed; and [a] high sense of public duties...*

A copy of this dedication was placed at the cornerstone of the new house. Like the theme of a symphony, the notes sounded in this dedicatory offering continue throughout the whole piece — the life of General Cocke. The new residence at Bremo was not just a home for the widower and his six children; it was like a temple of knowledge and compassion. It was built upon an act of remembrance and it was to be continued in the light of remembrance.

Born at Swann's Point, near Jamestown, on September 19, 1780, Cocke was fifth in the line of generation from the original settlers of the colony. He married Ann Blaws Barraud, a music student he met while attending the College of William and Mary, on Christmas Day in 1802. About 1809 the couple moved west, to Fluvanna County, to land granted to Cocke ancestors in 1725. In the war of 1812 Cocke became Brigadier-General, during which time, according to Cabell Moore, "he made a record for maintaining discipline and for taking care of his troops."

Ann Cocke died on December 27, 1816, three months after the birth of their last child. According to Cabell Moore, she wanted to be etched on her gravestone the statement that "it was she who first awakened her husband to a sense of the truth of Christianity."[1]

The General was engaged with the building of Bremo for about four years, from 1815-1819. This Palladian mansion, partially inspired by Jeffersonian architectural design, was later described by Samuel Eliot Morison and Henry Steele Commager in their *The Growth of the American Republic* (1950) as "perhaps the most beautiful country house in America today." To Fiske Kimball, "of all the houses in the Jeffersonian tradition, not even excepting Monticello, it is Bremo which makes the deepest impression of artistic perfection."[2]

The mansion communicates boldness and solemnity. A massive columned central brick building, each cardinal point flanked by a portico of Tuscan columns, is flanked by two wings, each of these a miniature Greek temple. In this design, the central mass with flanking connected wings, there is a sense of embrace and enclosure, a solidity not so much self-contained as welcoming. The temple has become a home. Classical Chronos, the devourer of his own children, has been Christianized –

What King is there but You who could
Give everlasting Good?[3]

General Cocke moved to Bremo with his family in 1819. A portion of his diary from this period — November 6, 1816, to May 19, 1818 — was typed up and made available to his descendants. Although he was concerned with the supervision of the building and execution of his plans, his diary is mostly the journal of the farmer and husbandman, full of details about the weather and crops: stemming and prizing tobacco, hauling manure, cutting ice, planting corn, shearing sheep, shocking rye, and the depredations of the Hessian fly.

But the diary describes movingly the progress of his wife's illness, first mention of which occurs on November 18, 1816:

---

[1] William Cabell Moore, "John Hartwell Cocke of Bremo," *William and Mary Quarterly Historical Magazine*, July, 1933.

[2] M. Boyd Coyner, *John Hartwell Cocke of Bremo: Agriculture and Slavery in the Antebellum South:* Ph.D. Dissertation, University of Virginia, 1961, p. 40. This work hereafter cited as "Coyner: Dissertation."

[3] "St. Ita's Vision," from *The Hermit Songs*, by Samuel Barber, G. Schirmer, Inc.

My neighbor, Robert Scott called on his way to Richmond, and by him I wrote to Doctor Everette requesting him to visit my wife, who continues to be in extremely ill health since the birth of our little Sally on the 8th of September.

For the next six weeks, regular entries detail the state of his wife's stomach, bowels, and soul:

November 26: Oh God! If it is my destiny to lose her, grant me fortitude under this heaviest of earthly afflictions!

December 5: My poor sick wife spent a wretched night. Altho she has been almost entirely relieved from the worst symptoms of the early stage of her disease, she complains of the most distressing state of feelings. She was watchful and uneasy all last night, and after frequently waking and taking some wine and water . . . at four o'clock in the morning she begged that I would come to her bed, saying that her feelings were indescribably distressing. Upon getting to her I found her pulse, I thought, more weak and frequent than I had ever before observed, and now for the first time her fortitude seemed to give way under the accumulated sufferings from her disease . . .

The couple take some consolation by reading the Gospel together.

In the course of the next few days Ann Cocke finds some relief through anodynes. By December 9 she is apparently more resigned to her situation, and by that time the diary breaks off from regular entries and becomes a recapitulation of her last days. She begins to make instructions for arrangements she wanted attended to upon her death, and with "angelic equanimity" reviews her past life with husband, children, friends, and servants.

During this heart-rending scene, while agonies of despair agitated every other bosom, she, for whose impending loss we grieved, was tranquil and composed, and frequently recalled our distracted minds back to a sense of duty and humble submission to the Will of God.

But when her son John returned home from school to see her, "the Saint, for a moment, gave way to the Mother, and she wept."

At about noon on Friday the 27th, "the last ebb of life commenced." Upon being told that her friend Mrs. Cabell was arriving in a carriage to see her, Ann Cocke said,

Is that the carriage I now hear . . . ? I can't wait for her.

She turned her head upon the pillow, and added –

I could not wait for any human being.

> *... By this time the power of speech was sensibly diminished... but she could still express herself intelligibly by signs ... After this she closed her eyes with her own hands, and still made us sensible that she was taking her last farewell of us by gentle pressure of her enfeebled hands. Finally such was the calm and peaceful rest of her blessed spirit, that it left her mortal remains without the slightest tremor of a nerve or the agitation of a muscle.*

* * *

In the period following his wife's death, Cocke's agricultural preoccupations resume. He notes in his diary the incidences of his meetings with Jefferson, Madison, Monroe, and others, on business having to do with the founding of the University of Virginia. On Sundays there is the weekly notation of devotions and a glimpse of his reading. On April 13th, 1817, a Sunday (Easter came on April 6 of that year) Cocke noted,

> *Read several of Sterne's sermons and an account of Doctor Johnson's death in Boswell's life of that distinguished man. A consolatory example of the efficiency of Christianity to impart comfort in that awful moment.*

On the day before that entry, on April 12, there is a telling passage:

> *... Attended a Regimental Muster at Nelson Court House... The tavern-keeper (Brooks) appeared to be in the first stages of consumption. Conversed with him about his health, which he seemed to think alarming. Experienced feelings very different from what I ever did before at conversing with a man who I thought hastening to the grave. They were not exactly feelings of envy, for I thought of the value of my life to my children, but they partook in no degree of that horror with which I had hitherto regarded such an object.*

The following month, on May 5, Cocke departed for Charlottesville, leaving Bremo on his horse at four o'clock in the morning and arriving at Monticello, Jefferson's home, at about 8:30 A.M. "Found the family just up from breakfast and the three illustrious gentlemen with whom I was to act waiting for my arrival," he writes. Mr. Jefferson he finds "as usual, easy and communicative," but also "serious and carried the marks of much care upon his brow." And: "Found Mr. Madison cheerful, communicative, and very fond of conversing on agricultural subjects — fortunately for me, that being the only subject upon which I had any chance of rendering myself at all interesting to a man of his superior acquirements and extensive knowledge."

The business of the University of Virginia consumed the next few days. Cocke returned to Monticello on May 7, from Charlottesville presumably, to dinner, and "to get the subscription papers which Mr. Jefferson had been preparing for promoting the College... Mr. Madison had left Monticello and the President (i.e., Mr. Monroe) had proceed'd also to Washington."

Cocke was detained at Monticello that night, for the final sentence in his journal entry for that day reads: "Was detained all night by rain at Monticello." He gives no mention of any conversation with Mr. Jefferson on that occasion, or indeed, even if Mr. Jefferson was there.

The brevity of the account conveys an enigmatic quality. The two men may not have had a substantive conversation then or perhaps at any time, given their differences in ages and, more pointedly, their differences in religious outlook. Dumas Malone, the biographer of Jefferson, wrote that "Jefferson once said that he rarely discussed religion and did so only in reasonable company."[4]

Not that General Cocke would not have been "reasonable company." But the two men belong to different generations. Mr. Jefferson at this time is seventy-three years of age, a man of the Enlightenment or Age of Reason, famous, former President and diplomat, author, agriculturalist, a man of prodigious talent, ingenuity, rationality.

General Cocke at this time is thirty-seven years old and is, in the words of one of his descendants, "an apostle of the new age of romanticism, spirituality, conflict, revolution, gothic, Sir Walter Scott, Christian revival, etc."[5] Recently widowed, he has an intelligent and sober disposition, and perhaps he is a bit in awe of his host.

Besides, there are different kinds of reason. Enlightenment reason is patterned on science, which aims to be impersonal or impartial. An important aspect of Christian reason is founded upon memory, which must lead through the personal if it is to bear fruit. These kinds of reason can be allies, but sometimes they are at war, or at least at odds, with a gulf between them not only of words but also of experience. [6]

In any event, it is known that by 1816-17 that Mr. Jefferson had completed the first draft of what would later be known as his 'Expurgated Bible.' This little book, *The Philosophy of Jesus*, attempted to distill from the New Testament a philosophy to which a rationalist like Jefferson could give his consent. In the Jefferson Bible all that was supernatural or miraculous was omitted from the Life of Jesus: it became a life of an ethical teacher, a life without the Story.

It is undeniable that General Cocke and Mr. Jefferson thought very differently about matters of religion. But whether there would have been an embargo on the subject between them is a matter of conjecture. It is not altogether impossible that Mr. Jefferson would have shown General Cocke his manuscript, nor impossible for the latter to have expressed an interest.

---

[4] Dumas Malone, *Jefferson and His Time: The Sage of Monticello*, Boston, 1981, p. 490.

[5] Letter, Joseph F. Johnston, Jr. to Caryl Johnston, 17 August 1994.

[6] I am generalizing here, not distinguishing the Scottish Enlightenment from its more general British (or French) forms. Even so, Henry F. May remarks that "Whatever has survived [i.e. of the Enlightenment] has had to be accommodated to the other and older source of American culture: Christianity in its myriad and shifting American forms." See his *The Enlightenment in America*, Oxford, 1976, p. 361.

Still — we can only guess, inferring the state of General Cocke's feelings, in which Christian faith is so important a part of the legacy of his deceased wife. A few years later, in 1825, we have some evidence as to what these feelings might have been. In a letter to his son John, Cocke wrote that "I would rather know that you were a disciple of the meek and lowly Jesus, and destined to pass your life in virtuous obscurity, than to have the assurance of your rising to the Presidency of the United States . . . and die an infidel."[7]

The allusion to Jefferson is pointed.

Interlude: A Conversation at Monticello

Two gentlemen sat up late on the night of May 7, 1817, conversing in the Library at Monticello. They have been discoursing upon a variety of topics but now it is late and the older man — he is seventy-three — says it is time for him to retire.

The younger man agrees that he must be off the first thing in the morning. "But I'd like to look over your **Philosophy of Jesus** *that you mentioned to me." The older man smiles in assent and goes to his desk, removes a sheaf of papers, and hands it to the younger man. They bid each other a cordial good night and the older man leaves the room.*

The young man peruses the papers, then sits brooding in silence for a long time. The glass of Muscat de Riversalle is half-finished; he does not touch it. He hears the steady beat of the rain upon the roof and thinks of his wife. He glances around the room, caught by a momentary feeling that she is present there with him. He imagines himself to be speaking and that she is listening.

"Mr. Jefferson and I disagree over everything that it is possible to disagree over, everything of importance, that is: about God, the nature of the Trinity, the supernatural, who Christ is, and whether the Resurrection really occurred."

He pauses, hearing nothing but the rain. He adds: "On general matters of ethics, however, we are more or less in accord." The rain continues to fall. His thoughts gather momentum and he says to himself, and to her, decisively: "But it is not possible to have the ethics without the story!"

He pauses as if to give her time to reply.

He recalls that Mr. Jefferson had said something to the effect that "It is in our lives and not our words that our religion must be read." And he answered: "This man does not hate the Gospel. But he does not understand it." It seemed to him that this thought was received willingly.

He rose from his chair and walked over to Mr. Jefferson's desk and placed the sheaf of papers there. The room was glowing in the candlelight and he felt reluctant to leave it just yet. Something was still pressing upon him to say or

---

[7] Coyner: Dissertation, p. 24. cf. also Cocke's remark to William Short in 1838: that [Christianity is] "the true secret, the *Summum bonum* of life."

think; ideas were quickening within him; he knew he had to pronounce something to relieve or turn away this host of presences.

"I will live this out," he finally announced, "and You must do something with what I have seen." With that he took a candlestick and turned, seeking the stairwell to the guest chamber. Before mounting the stairs he gave a short, swift knock on an inner door, and a sleepy servant came to put out the candles in the library and close the house for the night.
The General thanked him and bade him goodnight.

In the preceding I have placed myself as a witness to an imaginary conversation, an encounter between Jefferson and Cocke. At the time of this "conversation" General Cocke was thirty-seven years old. Thomas Jefferson was thirty-seven when he completed his manuscript, *Notes on the State of Virginia*, in which he made a number of aphoristic comments regarding religion, often quoted:

... it does me no injury for my neighbor to say there are twenty gods, or no god. It neither picks my pocket or breaks my leg.

Against government establishment of religion:

It is error alone which needs the support of government. Truth can stand by itself.

On Pennsylvania and New York, which abolished the established church:

They have made the happy discovery, that the way to
Silence religious disputes, is to take no notice of them.[8]

Merrill Peterson, the noted Jefferson scholar, wrote that "Unlike the anticlericalism of the Old World, Jefferson's hatred of priesthoods and establishments did not involve him in hatred of religion."[9]

This may be true, but it does not get to the heart of the problem. Truth, for Jefferson, is something impersonal — it can "stand by itself." But Christian truth is historical. Three roads came together when Hebrew memory took a journey through Greek thinking and ended up in Roman history. The encounter at the three roads made a whole new world, which our Gothic ancestors expressed in their word for *world*: *wer+eld*, the 'man-age,' or 'age of man.'

This new world, in which time and man were joined, could work as long as the Creator stood in the beginning and the Judgment waited at the end. In

---

[8] Thomas Jefferson, *Notes on the State of Virginia*, University of North Carolina Press, 1954, p. 159-161.
[9] Peterson, "Jefferson and Religious Freedom," *Atlantic Monthly*, Dec. 1994.

this *wer-eld*, truth is the one thing that cannot "stand alone." It is supported by a multiplicity of relationships having to do with the stages of realization, the "means" of thinking. We cannot altogether fault Jefferson for failing to understand this; after all, many Christians forgot it too. In any case, the Christians might have done better to hold fast to the things that remained — the Beginning and the End.

They did not — whence the terrific energies devoted to quarrels, sects, and establishments — and the collapse of the End and the Beginning has given rise to the problem of *meaningless truth*. It is significant that in Jefferson's 'Expurgated Bible,' almost the entire Gospel of John was expunged. For in that Gospel is the teaching of the Word on the way to becoming fact. It is the Gospel of the *means*.

Twentieth-century America has embraced Jeffersonianism in religion. For some people today, this presents no great calamity. But those of us in the rearguard do engage at times in anxious thought, one of them having to do with the relationship of thinking to the rest of human nature. Thinking can roll along quite well on wheels of intellect, and a great destiny, like Jefferson's, can be the result. But it is not a *Christian* destiny. It is incumbent upon us, anxious thinkers that we are, to show why this is so, and why it might be important.

* * *

The concept of developmental stages is essential to the study of spiritual biography. For General Cocke, I suggested that at thirty-seven, when this "conversation" with Mr. Jefferson occurred, he gained an insight into Mr. Jefferson's relationship to Christianity as well as into his own future destiny. *"I will live this out,"* Cocke said— in my poetic reconstruction — *"and You must do something with what I have seen."*

Who is this "You" here? Christ? His own higher self? The spirit of his late wife? The witnesses of history?   I leave the question unanswered, for the episode of which it forms the conclusion is neither historically accurate nor historically impossible. It falls within the range, the realm, of Story. As the historian John Lukacs once remarked, something does not need to be a fact in order to be true.[10] I have taken the Old General's brief, unembellished lines — "Was detained all night by rain at Monticello," — and formed them into a story.

Perhaps the General willingly consented that night to a form of sacrifice. It was perhaps a sacrifice of intellectualism — which, though it can be a form of discipline, can also lead to a kind of luxuriance, or enjoyment. The Old General was too frugal for that — this "puritan cavalier" (according to

---

[10] His words: "...the problem of truth is not necessarily a problem of fact." *Historical Consciousness*, New York, 1985, p. 108.

Clement Eaton) had a great deal of the puritan and less of the cavalier in his nature. Ideas are a necessity. But to be lived out they must be few in number.

To become productive ideas need to be realized. Not only must they become capable of meeting the logic of reason; they must be able to meet the illogic of life. Truly productive ideas are few in number.

Perhaps General Cocke's interior meditation at Monticello had to do with this realization about the nature of ideas, and what such a realization would mean to his own life. For only a few ideas are worth putting into practice. To these Cocke said: I will live this out. With this deed the widower became the husbandman of Christian revelation.

* * *

Biography that takes account of the interior life emphasizes the significance of developmental stages in human life. One of these stages occurs every eighteen years, in an interval sometimes called the moon nodes. The moon node correlates with a lunar interval, when the moon, crossing the ecliptic, "returns to the same position relative to the earth and sun it had when the human being was born."[11] Such times are often turning points. According to Diether Lauenstein, it is at the second moon node (the 37th year) that there can be an experience of "sacrifice, expulsion, or death."

I was struck, in studying the biography of General John Hartwell Cocke, by the events that occurred at roughly eighteen-year intervals.

Ann Cocke died just as General Cocke was entering his thirty-seventh year. According to Boyd Coyner, whose doctoral dissertation on Cocke has been indispensable to this account, it was at one point in the year 1817 that Cocke felt himself to be at the point of death. He drafted a will explaining why he was not freeing his slaves at this time.

But the subject of slavery was evidently very much on his mind. In 1817 the American Colonization Society was formed, and Cocke became an active member. The goals of this Society were to emancipate slaves and pay for their passage to Liberia. Coyner dates this shift "from planter to apostle of uplift" from 1817. Eighteen years later, in 1834-35, Cocke was on the verge of embarking on his most ambitious experiment in emancipation. It involved the purchase of lands in the Deep South and a practical emancipation program. The fruits of this experiment became apparent by 1852 — again, another interval of eighteen years. At that time Cocke accompanied three emancipated slaves to New Orleans, where he bid them farewell as they were about to take passage on a steamer bound for Liberia.

There are many passages in human life, and I do not single out the eighteen-year interval as the only one or one possessing unique importance. For reasons I do not understand, the eighteen-year interval struck me when

---

[11] Diether Lauenstein, *Biblical Rhythms in Biography*, Floris Books, Edinburgh, 1974.

studying General Cocke's biography. I can only suggest that perhaps at the eighteen-year interval the temporal soul meets with the eternal spirit in a particular way, and that the deeds carried out at these times have a particular significance.[12]

* * *

In 1966 the subject of American slavery revisited the public mind with the publication of William Styron's novel, *The Confessions of Nat Turner*. This book had considerable interest to the descendants of General Cocke. Some time previously, one of the Cocke cousins, upon being introduced to Styron, brought the journals of John Hartwell Cocke to the author's attention. A fictionalized General Cocke appears in the portrait of the kind master, Samuel Turner, whose very words — that slavery "is a cancer eating at the vitals of the Commonwealth" — were penned by the Old General in 1832.

But the kind master of the novel, who in the end, and not out of malice, betrays his slave, comes across as a far less complex figure than his original. Though just and humane, Turner lacks the dimension of moral struggle so evident in Cocke. Most especially he lacks religion. In the novel, religion is relegated to the black slaves and a few marginal whites.

The omission speaks volumes, and at least where General Cocke is concerned, it is inaccurate. The Old General devoted upwards of four decades of his life to the Christian evangelization, instruction, and conversion of his slaves, not to mention his efforts to encourage strong family life, the practice of virtue, and abstention from alcohol. "I cannot conceive how anyone who acknowledges the common obligations of Christian duty" [could shirk the responsibility of imparting religious teaching to his slaves] "unless he degrades them to a rank below humanity and denies their possessing immortal souls,"[13] Cocke wrote in 1834.

One of the results of the slave insurrection in Southampton, Virginia, in 1831, led by Nat Turner, was that the Virginia legislature passed a law prohibiting the salaried employment of whites to teach slaves to read and write.

General Cocke spoke bitterly to the end of his life about the folly of this law — "the monument of our shame." In order to circumvent it, his wife Louisa, (in 1821 Cocke married, for the second time, a widow, Mrs. Louisa Maxwell Holmes[14]) commenced teaching the rudiments of learning in the

---

[12] Lauenstein says that at the second moon node there begins a "partial freeing of soul-forces" and a placing of oneself before "the objective spirit of the world."

[13] Coyner: Dissertation, p. 325.

[14] According to Coyner, the General was attracted to Mrs. Holmes "because of her exemplary standing in the Presbyterian Church." Coyner remarked that Louisa brought "a puritan temper of pervasive pertinacity," but speaks highly of her mental acquirements.

infant school for the slaves on the plantation, a task she continued for four or five years.

The educational efforts were an integral part of the General's plan for slave emancipation. To free the slave without having provided him an education, a trade, or a means to earn his living would be, Cocke thought, a cruelty almost as bad as bondage itself. At times deeply discouraged by the slow pace of educational attainment and moral reform — an act of reciprocity he considered the necessary prior condition for emancipation — Cocke nevertheless believed that the barriers were cultural rather than racial. In 1855 he wrote that, given the circumstances, "Would the Anglo-Saxon race have done any better?"

The 1830's were boom times in the cotton lands of the Deep South — Alabama and Mississippi. In the middle of that decade Cocke conceived of a plan to turn cotton profits to the worthy purpose of slave emancipation. His idea was to purchase land in that region, transport some of his slaves there, and have them work to earn funds for their own independence.

"The General's plan was nobly conceived and had the businessman's touch of practicality," writes Coyner.[15]

On February 10, 1840, forty-nine slaves and nine horses and mules departed Bremo for Alabama on what was to begin a twenty-one year experiment, brought to a close only with the onset of the Civil War. Coyner writes that nothing quite like it had ever before been attempted in the South. Although some other Southern planters had experimented with similar schemes, Cocke's program for emancipation was a unique blend: the participation of the slave in a financial sense as well as a moral, and an education for citizenship involving right conduct and productivity.

Nay-sayers there were, including Cocke's own son-in-law, Nathaniel Francis Cabell, who warned him that it would not work. Coyner writes that in 1835 "Cocke was warned that a Fluvanna candidate for the legislature had sworn to beat him on sight." He believes that Cocke may have suffered violence, noting that the pages of Louisa Cocke's diary have been "significantly if maddeningly cut out" in the relevant period. When the entries resume a few days later, Louisa made reference to her poor sick husband and to "the late scenes...[that] appear like a troubled dream from which I have not fully awaked."[16]

There is an intriguing sequel to this story. While on a visit to Bremo on the weekend of August 14, 1994, I was sitting in the library with my cousin, Joseph Johnston, Jr. We had been discussing this incident in the life of General Cocke some time before. Joe had then begun reading Thomas Scott's *Holy Bible* (Philadelphia, 1812), vol. 4. He noted some marginal notes in the hand of John Hartwell Cocke:

---

[15] Coyner: Dissertation, p. 378.
[16] Coyner: Dissertation, p. 350.

Friday October 16th 1835
The day of the deepest humiliation of my life.
May God in his mercy help me in this sore trial.

And in pencil, hard to read:

God has answered my [prayer?] and permitted me to rejoice in his service.

Whether or not these notes refer to an incident of violence against Cocke can only be guessed. *Something* happened and was recorded in that Bible and remembered in that room. Here was an epiphany of Southern remembrance — where, so often, as Flannery O'Connor put it, "the violent bear it away."

* * *

Clement Eaton described Cocke as a "puritan cavalier. . . strikingly free from intolerance. He received *Uncle Tom's Cabin* with sympathy, as a work destined to hasten the fall of slavery."[17]

Cocke read and admired Harriet Beecher Stowe's work and even attempted to pay a visit to Mrs. Stowe on one of his visits to the North. He was no ally of the abolitionists, however, whom he regarded as fanatics at a safe distance from the problem. He would have agreed with Stanley Elkins' judgment of them: "The very nature of that thought — anti-institutional, individualistic, abstract, and charged with guilt — blocked off all concrete approaches to the problems of society."[18]

According to Elkins, the very decentralized, even atomized, nature of American life at the time offered no impediment to the reformist zeal of the abolitionists: there was no established church, no national university, no national focus of social or mercantile interests, no national bar. Hence: "... the intellectual without connections, chronically the case in America" — the reformer with no stake in society. With respect to the problem of slavery, Elkins adds: "The true difficulty lay in the absence of any sense of *limits* within which the problem would have to be handled, limits functioning to exhibit not only the impossible but also the possible."[19]

Cocke was pre-eminently a man of connections, but in his struggle to discover the limits he acted very much as a man alone. In retrospect it is easy to ridicule an emancipatory effort which resulted, in the end, in the emancipation of fewer than twenty slaves. Such meager results seem to vindicate the attitude of the modern liberal, who condemns a venture in which "you had to prove you were worthy of freedom by being a good slave."

---

[17] Clement Eaton, *Freedom of Thought in the Old South*, Duke University Press, 1940, p. 10-11.
[18] Stanley Elkins, *Slavery*, University of Chicago, 1959, p. 206.
[19] Elkins, *op.cit.*, p. 194.

This is a sneer — certainly an attitude not characteristic of this individual, the best of her kind [20] - because liberalism runs the danger of taking civilization for granted.

Contrast my liberal friend's attitude with the sober realism of William the Silent, founder of the Dutch Republic: "It is not necessary to hope in order to undertake, nor to succeed in order to persevere." Freedom is not the root of civilization but its fruit, and the work that needs to take place below the soil is the perennial, repeated problem of man, born anew with every newborn child. The ongoing work of civilization is the lost term in the liberal syllogism.

Efforts like those of General Cocke's were vindicated by Stanley Elkins, however. What was needed to deal with the problem of slavery, he said, were bridges of "institutional leverage" to exert "claims upon society" — a "myriad of intermediate relationships." [21]

We have met with before this concern for the means, the intermediate step. It is an important idea in Christianity, but one which for the most part has not been emphasized in Christian teaching. It is best preserved in the stories of the Holy Grail. "Grail" derives from *gradalis,* step or stage, 'gradual.' In Cocke's emancipation program, the *gradalis* or idea of intermediate stages becomes the paradigm for moral reform that actually achieves the level of *deed.*[22]

There is no indication by Stanley Elkins that he knew of the efforts of General Cocke. But he might have been describing these efforts when he said that what the South needed were planters who educated their slaves, "law or no law," — and who Christianized them, "ridicule or no ridicule" and who let them work for their own independence. [23]

Only at the end of his life did the Old General change his mind with respect to slavery. He recanted his earlier anti-slavery views, basing his new arguments on the Abrahamic Covenant, the patriarch who safeguards the welfare

---

[20] This came from Virginia Durr, author of *Outside the Magic Circle* (1985), a Southern liberal and friend of the Cocke and Johnston families. Her remark about General Cocke expresses the fundamental weakness of liberalism. It assumes that freedom exists in the abstract apart from the problem of civilization. It was a weakness of liberal thought of which Virginia was generally aware, but seemed not to be so in this case.

[21] Elkins, p. 198. Compare with Vaclav Havel "On the Responsibility of Intellectuals" — "Seeking to improve it (i.e., the world) people should proceed with the utmost caution and sensitivity, step by step, always paying attention to what each change actually brings about." *New York Review of Books,* June 22, 1995.

[22] In this respect it is useful to remember Stanley Elkins' discussion of abolitionism in relation to transcendentalism. He says: "It has been...asserted... that the most notable intellectual expression of the 1830's and 1840's in the United States — Transcendentalism — was quite unable... to 'transcend' its culture and age at all: that is, far from 'revolting' against the age, Transcendentalism embodied in aggravated form certain of its most remarkable features — its anti-institutionalism, its individual perfectionism, its abstraction, and its guilt and reforming zeal. Moreover, the intellectual feature of the reform movement most relevant to this inquiry — abolitionism — very strikingly duplicated those very features just enumerated, particularly guilt and its counterpart, moral aggression." *Slavery,* p. 158.

[23] Coyner: Dissertation, p. 449.

of his people. His change of heart and alliance with the Southern cause may be understandable due to the stresses of war and the infirmities of old age. In addition there was the suicide of his son, Philip St. George Cocke, in 1861. Boyd Coyner remarks that the Old General never referred to this blow in any of his writings. Whatever the General's feelings may have been are hidden behind a veil of silence. Coyner also notes that Douglas Southall Freeman gave substantial credit to Philip St. George Cocke for engineering the victory at First Manassas. Apparently Philip broke under the strain of command. [24]

---

[24] "My guess is that the problem of honor had something to do with it. He didn't get the credit and seniority he felt he deserved." Editorial note, Joseph F. Johnston, Jr.

Philip St. George Cocke.
Portrait at Bremo.

Ann Blaws Barraud Cocke.
Portrait at Bremo Recess. Courtesy: Raymond Orf

III. The Blooded Colt

At age twenty-nine John Hartwell Cocke wrote his friend Joseph Carrington Cabell:

> "I have already planned a division of my time between my Farms, my Garden & my Books ... When all things are snug upon the Farms & I get seated before a good fire in my little study with my Wife by my side & the sweet voices of our playing children now & then breaking upon my Ear... I would not exchange situations with the most puissant prince of the House of Napoleon." [1]

About six years had passed since John and Nancy Cocke had left the Tidewater for Central Virginia. The young couple with their growing family evidently had much to be happy about. Armistead Gordon, Jr., who wrote the biographical entry for General Cocke in the *Dictionary of American Biography*, and whose own biography of Cocke unfortunately was never completed, describes the courtship of John Cocke and Ann Barraud as pretty much along the lines of 'they only had eyes for each other.' He dwells with some affection on Ann (or Nancy) Barraud Cocke:

> "Nancy's first letter to her parents from Bremo, after they had made the move, breathes serenity and contentment, even while it gives us a glimpse into that generous tenderness of spirit which characterized so many Southern women of the Antebellum era — but which is now too often regarded as a trait gratuitously bestowed upon their heroines by imaginative romancers nostalgic for the 'good old days.' " [2]

---

[1] John Hartwell Cocke to J.C. Cabell, Bremo, Dec. 26, 1809. Cabell Papers, University of Virginia.

[2] Armistead Gordon Papers, Draft for Cocke Biography, Unpublished Mss., no page numbers. University of Virginia.

Ann Blaws Barraud, born Dec. 25, 1784, easily conquered the heart of her husband's future biographer. Mr. Gordon continues:

> "It is scarcely possible to read the letters written by her more than a century ago without coming under the spell of her natural wholesomeness and sweetness. Considerate, gentle, generous, responsive, self-effacing, she made friends easily and kept them..." [3]

The Cockes appear to have been in agreement regarding their mode of life together. One of the results of General Cocke's military career in the War of 1812 was that certain friends suggested that he seek political office. While her husband was on military duty, Ann Cocke wrote to him:

> "You think as I would have you on the subject... Surely I would feel flattered by seeing you distinguished in any way, but our happiness has been marked out so differently that I would not think it wise to exchange . . . a situation which would so completely pull down the foundation we have built on."[4]

That foundation was that of domestic life, marriage, estate management, and raising children to take their place in the social order. Had Ann Cocke not died on the eve of her thirty-third year, leaving her spouse devastated, her six children motherless, and her parents and kin in Norfolk grief-stricken, it is probable that this purely private life would have continued.

> Or would it? Such a question is impossible to answer. How a person responds to life's unpredictable turns marks him as a fatalist, a cynic, an agnostic. Those we call Christian are those who are able to receive the *gift of death*. [5]

The source of Ann Cocke's Christian convictions remains unclear. She wanted it to be remembered on her gravestone that it was she who had awakened her husband to the truths of Christianity. After her death, when the grief-stricken husband had begun to find the consolation of religion, there is a letter to him from his father-in-law, Dr. Barraud, to the effect that such a consolation was not available to him or to Ann's mother. The Barrauds do not appear to have been especially religious or pious by nature. Nor did Cocke lean much in that direction prior to Ann's death. Armistead Gordon remarks that, "His

---

[3] Armistead Gordon Papers, Cocke Biography, University of Virginia.

[4] Armistead Gordon Papers, Cocke Biography, University of Virginia.

[5] "Jesus...proved that every end could and should be turned into a new beginning, that even absolute failure and death could be made fertile. Herewith the last frontier of the soul was conquered...Death became carrier of life *between* souls." Eugen Rosenstock-Huessy, *The Christian Future*, New York, 1946, p. 66-67.

was not a reflective cast of mind. . . Neither with Nancy nor with their friends do spiritual topics appear to have loomed large in his conversation."[6]

But already by March, 1817, a few short months after Nancy's death the previous December, we sense that change is afoot. Cocke is writing about his wife's death and his discovery of Christianity to Judge St. George Tucker in Williamsburg: "I have had the consolation to say, that at every step in my progress of investigating revealed religion, my doubts and difficulties have diminished and my hopes of perfect conviction have brightened. " [7]

Whether Ann Cocke's Christian faith resulted from her sufferings in health, or whether it pre-dated her illness, remains a matter of conjecture. More biographical information on Ann Cocke would be needed to research this question in her case.

But even were further research to be carried out, my guess would be that Ann Cocke was one of those "naturally Christian" souls — *anima naturaliter christiana*.

I argue first from dates. Ann Cocke was born on Christmas Day, 1784; she was married on Christmas Day, 1802. She died during the Christmas season, Dec. 27, 1816. She was a child of the "Twelve Holy Nights." This period, from December 24th to January 6th of every year, carries with it a certain spiritual *éclat*. There is the Scandinavian legend of Olaf Astesen, who fell asleep during this period and was granted visions of the cosmos and the heavenly beings — a forerunner, perhaps, of our more secular Rip Van Winkle.

Perhaps Ann Cocke is an American representative of the feminine aspect of the Holy Spirit. This mysterious third aspect of the Trinity has sometimes been known as "Sophia," or Wisdom. A "sophianic" brand of Christianity has arisen in recent years in some New Age circles, with not always beneficial results. Yet the psychologist Karl Stern wrote an interesting critique of modern rationalism, *The Flight from Woman,* in which he pointed out the derivation of "Sophia" from *sapere,* to taste. The book argued that extreme rationalism may indicate a rejection of the feminine and of the primordial trust-experience of tasting, suckling, and receiving.

That such notions have been distorted by feminism — one of the most rationalistic doctrines ever invented — is unfortunate. In any case, the conversion experience of the "Sophia" type seems to be less well known in Christian history. It seems different from the conversion experienced by St. Paul, for example. The conversion of Paul is dramatic; his whole soul is turned inside out. He becomes literally a 'new man,' even to the point of changing his name. Cocke's conversion appears to be more gradual and metamorphic. Perhaps it is not so much a 'new man' as a deeper one that this type of experience makes possible.

---

[6] Armistead Gordon Papers, Cocke Biography, University of Virginia.

[7] Armistead Gordon Papers, Cocke Biography, University of Virginia.

Whatever Cocke encountered in his dark night of the soul brought on by grief, love, and loss, it was as deep as it was lasting. His subsequent actions appear only to extend, deepen, and fructify this initial experience.

That General Cocke had a conversion is confirmed, though not in those words, by Frank Edgar Grizzard, who wrote his Master's thesis on General Cocke. He quotes a passage from the Funeral Sermon for General Cocke that was preached by C. Tyree and published in the Richmond *Religious Herald* in 1866:

> *I learned from him orally that he became a Christian soon after the death of his first wife. 'I had,' said he, in an interview in regard to his conversion, 'seen an end to all perfection. I had had my share of wealth and worldly honors, but when God took from me the early companion of my bosom I realized that all such things were vanity and vexation of spirit. When the crushing blow came, I repined under the chastening hand of God. I was, however, soon taught by grace the rebellion and wickedness of my heart, and then, I trust, I was led by repentance and faith to Christ.'* [8]

I turn, then, to the question: what sort of Christian religion did General Cocke adhere to? This question will occupy the bulk of this chapter, in which I will quote passages from those of the Old General's letters and journals that I have been able to peruse. He will speak for himself.

Before doing this, however, I would like to call attention to an incident mentioned by Dumas Malone, the biographer of Jefferson, and also by Armistead Gordon. It concerns General Cocke's role in the founding of the University of Virginia. It was a role primarily confined to the auditing of funds and the construction of the physical campus, says Gordon. But there were other things as well of a more intangible nature, and Cocke's influence cannot be discounted.

General Cocke was one of six members of the Board of Visitors (the founding body of the University) the other five being Thomas Jefferson, James Madison, James Monroe, Joseph Carrington Cabell of Nelson County, and David Watson of Louisa County. By 1819, most political and legislative hurdles having been passed, Mr. Jefferson wanted to open for classes. The buildings were not yet finished. Cocke regarded the plan to open as premature — his word is "injudicious." There was also the matter of Dr. Thomas Cooper, whom Mr. Jefferson wanted to hire to teach a dazzling array of sciences. [9] To

---

[8] From Frank Edgar Grizzard, *'A Perilous and Grievous Burden' The Dilemma of the Antislavery Slaveholder in Virginia During the Early National Period: A Case Study of General John Hartwell Cocke*, Master's thesis, University of Virginia, May, 1989. Grizzard also mentions elsewhere that Ann Cocke spoke about Cocke's affectionate nature as a husband. He quotes her as saying she was "happy as a wife."

[9] To wit, zoology, chemistry, botany, mineralogy, and anatomy. Thomas Cooper (1759-1839), an Englishman, was nominated to the Royal Society by his friend Joseph Priestley but his radical

Jefferson, Thomas Cooper was a "paragon of learning," and his anti-clerical views were also to Mr. Jefferson's liking. The University of Virginia, founded by Jefferson, was one of the first universities in America to be founded without an official tie to any church. Dr. Cooper had little use for religious orthodoxy and he was not afraid of publishing his views. He was, as Malone remarked, an "inveterate controversialist." [10]

According to Armistead Gordon, "Cocke and Cabell were decidedly lukewarm about employing the talented by impolitic Cooper, whose religious opinions ran counter to public opinion in Virginia and this not merely among the more vocal denominations." [11]

There was a meeting of the Board of Visitors on March 1, 1819, which, according to Malone, adopted Jefferson's proposals regarding the building plans but refused any action concerning faculty appointments. Malone remarks that there appears to have been no criticism of Cooper's religious views at this stage.

Although it seems that General Cocke received letters from a Presbyterian clergyman warning him against Thomas Cooper's hostility to religious orthodoxy *after* this March 1 meeting, what he had heard of Cooper's heterodoxy by that point was not to his liking. What proportion of Cocke's dissent may be attributed to unfinished buildings and what proportion to his reservations about Cooper, is difficult to say. But he made a stand. In a letter to Cabell he described what it cost him:

> "... the thought of opposing my individual opinion upon a subject of this nature against the high authority of Mr. J[efferson] and Mr. M[adison] has cost me a conflict which has shaken the very foundations of my health..."[12]

Armistead Gordon makes the pertinent observation that it was Cocke and Cabell who seemed to be mainly the ones to place some restraints upon Mr. Jefferson's enthusiasms. In the matter of Dr. Thomas Cooper, even Cabell wrote that "Mr. Jefferson has gone too far." Cocke, no doubt still shaken from having made a principled opposition to the wishes of the Grey Eminence, no doubt agreed.

* * *

---

views made him unacceptable to that body. He was a "materialist in philosophy, a Unitarian in theology, and a revolutionist in political theory...His various anti-clerical pamphlets are far from philosophical, but are extremely interesting as an expression of aggressive modernism." *Dictionary of American Biography*, IV,414-15.

[10] See Dumas Malone, *The Sage of Monticello,* Boston, 1981, esp. 365-380 for exposition of the Cooper controversy and Cocke's role in it.

[11] Armistead Gordon Papers, Cocke Biography, University of Virginia.

[12] JHC to Joseph C. Cabell, 1 March 1819, Cabell Mss., 38-111, University of Virginia. I reproduce this letter in full in an Appendix to this chapter.

In his Journal of 1852, the Old General begins in January with the re-dedication of his life:
"... that I may say with the patriarch in the Bible, as for me and my House, the first desire of my heart is that we shall serve thee, Oh Lord."

It would have been easier to depart this life sooner, he says, but

"May it be that Thou will use me as the instrument of the conversion of the children thou hast given me: that I may see before my departure hence the full triumph of the temperance reformation —African Colonization — the Bible cause & a revival of Religion at the University of Va. — for all of which I have so long prayed..."[13]

In 1854 he notes joyfully that thirty students at the University made a public profession of faith:

"<u>Wonderful</u>, considering all the circumstances with which I am acquainted touching this Institution from its foundation —the cornerstone of which I assisted in [laying] — the most remarkable event in the History of Virginia. It is a signal of the times among many others that Christ's Kingdom upon Earth predicted in Scripture is approaching ..."[14]

In that year, 1852, Cocke's grandson P. B. Cabell converted to the Swedenborg church, also called the New Jerusalem Church. Immanuel Swedenborg was a visionary philosopher, according to Cocke, "whom much learning hath made mad."[15]

Yet the Old General himself almost talks Swedenborgian language of the heavenly New Jerusalem when he calls for a platform to sustain Christian Union, that shall be "*... so broad & firm for the New Jerusalem of the Apocalypse.*"[16]

Perhaps here Cocke was echoing the sentiments of Bishop James Madison (cousin of the president) who was president of the College of William and

---

[13] This and previous passage from the Journal of John Hartwell Cocke, # 640, Box 188, University of Virginia.

[14] Journal 1854, Cocke Papers, Box 188, University of Virginia.

[15] Swedenborg, [1688-1772] a scientist, claimed to have clairvoyant experiences of the spiritual world. He conversed with the Dead and mounted an ambitious defense of Christianity against atheists, deists, and rationalists. He believed in the primacy of the Imagination and that man's condition was determined by his 'intention' —i.e., his love. Cocke's daughter, Ann Blaws Cocke, married Nathaniel Francis Cabell on September 14, 1831. N. F. Cabell became a devout convert to Swedenborgianism; there were some tensions with Gen. Cocke and his second wife in this matter. In 1844 Cocke wrote of the Swedenborgians: "Alas by how many paths men seek to find out a way of their own to Heaven rather than the Highway marked out by Christ." Journal, 1844, Cocke Papers, University of Virginia.

[16] Journal, 1854, Cocke Papers, Box 188, University of Virginia.

Mary from 1777-1812. Cocke was a student there during this period. Bishop Madison taught Moral Philosophy and believed that all professing Christians should unite into one church. In any case General Cocke does not appear to be preoccupied with denominationalism. While on a trip to Alabama in 1844, he records that he had a conversation with a black Christian. Cocke goes with him to his church. *"He was curious to find out to what Church I belonged — but was quite satisfied with the [answer?] that I loved without respect to names equally all who truly loved the Lord Jesus Christ."* [17]

Nor does the Old General seem to take any satisfaction with excessive praying: *"The more I see of the long Prayer Book services, even with all the beauty & force of the Litany, [...] the more I am made to think of our Lord's protest against 'too much speaking.' Long prayers — his own divine model being not 60 seconds long — and as to the priestly costume — there being in the Bible no warrant for it."*[18]

The Old General scatters his exhortations liberally. On action: *"He who waits for great occasions to act, may possibly pass thru' life and not act at all — but God has graciously promised his approbation 'to the [doing?] of small things'..."*[19]

On the sustenance of political liberty, which he recognizes to be Christian morality — the American Bible Society and the American Tract Society, he says, *"do more for the future prosperity of our country than all the political machinery under the Constitution."*[20]

On salvation: *"The argument in favor of free grace & the inability of the sinner to do anything for his salvation I humbly concur is carried too far, when it omits the willingness & anxiety of the sinner to be saved... I believe God condescends thus far to be a co-worker with his creatures in 'working out their own salvation.' The absolute <u>exclusion</u> from all participation in the work leads to fatalism."*[21]

The Old General was a horse-lover from his earliest days. Armistead Gordon remarks that for a man so little given to self-indulgence, this fondness for horses and horse-racing is surprising. Randall Miller comments that "Cocke's horses enjoyed a local reputation for speed; indeed, one of his horses figured prominently in a celebrated escape story during the first months of Union occupation in Alabama. According to local legend, a Confederate veteran who murdered a federal soldier sped away to safety on a Cocke thoroughbred mare." [22]

Surprising or not, the Old General finds in horsemanship one of his most powerful religious metaphors:

---

[17] Journal, 1844, Cocke Papers, Box 188, University of Virginia.
[18] Journal, 1854, Sept. Cocke Papers, Box 188, University of Virginia.
[19] JHC to Charles Cocke, Dec. 5, 1844. Cocke Papers, University of Virginia.
[20] Journal, 1853, May 12. Cocke Papers, Box 188, University of Virginia.
[21] Journal, 1855, Dec. 22. Cocke Papers, Box 188, University of Virginia.
[22] Randall Miller, *Dear Master: Letters of a Slave Family,* Georgia, 1990, p.170 (footnote 2).

"Let it not be said, that the vocations of life, may all be abandoned under too strict exactions of Christian conformity — the requirement to pray always, does not mean that we must always be upon our knees . . . And dedicating our callings to God we may naturally in the current of business send up successive aspirations to Heaven for grace & favor upon our employment . . . [But] Who for example would think of presenting his blooded colt, in his prayers to God & ask that he might grow up & make a distinguished performer on the Turf? ...
... the regenerated Man classes his blooded colt with the rest of his stock . . ." [23]

---

[23] Journal, 1855, Dec. 1. Cocke Papers, University of Virginia.

John Hartwell Cocke, 1850
Bremo Recess Papers
Courtesy: Frances Orf

Appendix to Chapter Three

J.H. Cocke to Joseph C. Cabell, of the Senate, Richmond. Joseph Carrington Cabell (1778-1856) was a member of the Virginia Senate from 1810-1829, and again served in the House of Delegates from 1831-35. He served the University for thirty-seven years, as visitor and rector.

From The Cabell Papers, Accession 38-111, Box 13, Special Collections Department, University of Virginia. With notes by Cabell: "Meeting of Visitors of Central College — appointment of Dr. Cooper — [opposed?] ..." General Cocke's handwriting is generally flowing and legible, though there is an occasional word difficult to decipher. A seal or smudge mark obscures one or two other words.

Bremo 1st March 1819
My dear Cabell,
    I feel somewhat uneasy at not hearing from you in answer to my last replying to yours of the 1st & 4 Febry. Reports which have reached us represent your health to be recovering. I was quite gratified to receive Mr. Jeffersons accounts upon this subject but I afterward found he derives his information from a letter of the same date as my last from you. Do let me hear from you immediately. Say whether you go to the Lower Country before the meeting of the visitors & at any rate when I shall see you.
    You are already informed that Mr. J— called a meeting of the Visitors of Central College under the [Clause?] of the Univer[*smudge*] continuing our [powers?] until the 1st meeting of the University Visitors.[1] The time was

---

[1] A new Board of Visitors was appointed, their first meeting having been scheduled for March 29, 1819. The March 1 meeting was the last meeting of the old Board. Cocke was also appointed to the new Board.

Monday last & the place Mr. Madisons. Watson was prevented from attending by the bad weather and I only met Mr. J and Mr. M — and in the whole course of my life, never have I encountered a severer trial. Knowing that the progress of the building would be materially retarded if there was no meeting before the 29 March, I went up expecting only that subjects connected with this object would be presented to the meeting — but Mr. J had previously arranged a plan not only for this purpose, but for the election of Dr. Cooper to fill the professorships & go into immediate operation without a coadjutor in any other branch of the sciences. Such a step at this period — seemed to me to be so injudicious for a variety of reasons, that I felt myself bound to withhold my assent to it — and the thought of opposing my individual opinion upon a subject of this nature against the high authority of Mr. J. & Mr. M. has cost me a conflict which has shaken the very foundations of my health (for I feel now as if I should have a spell of illness) but I could not act otherwise, for the convictions of my judgment were so clear — that if I had expired under the trial I would have held out to the last. From something that dropt from Mr. J. after he had withdrawn the propositions in relation to Cooper I am induced to infer that you would have supported me in the course I took in this business & that he was in possession of this information. Should it be the case, do hasten to give me all the consolation you can on the subject, for even now, when I think of what I have done, I am half inclined to suppose it temerity.— I am too unwell to write you a detailed account of the views which actuated me in the affair. Especially as we shall so soon meet. [Suffice?] it for the present to say, that after that part of the project in relation to [*seal or smudge*] appointment was withdrawn everything went on smoothly and I could not discover that my opposition to this part of the plan has excited the least displeasure.

Perhaps my present feelings of indisposition are somewhat increased by riding the greater part of the day on Thursday last, which was here one of the most snowing days we have had this winter. I thought this was a little enterprising in a man of my age, but when I reached Col. Lindsays in the Eveng and found that Mr. Jefferson on the verge of 76 had left that plan in the morning and gone to Mr. Madison's 12 miles on Horse back thro' the weather I resigned all pretensions upon this score. I have the pleasure to inform you, that his health has recovered most rapidly of late — there is scarcely now a vestige remaining of his last alarming illness.

I did not get home until last last eveng and have not had time to look into last weeks papers and therefore know nothing of what the legislation has been about of late — this added to my indisposition must be my apology for saying nothing on the topic of public affairs.

Present me most cordially to our friend Coalter & his children and for yourself & Cousin Polly be assured of my warmest affection.
JHCocke

IV. Soldier of the Cross

i. Law of Generations

In the Old Testament there is a story that tells of the crisis-point between the generations. It depicts with terrifying accuracy the passing of the torch, when the younger generation takes over from the older. This story of the Sacrifice, or Binding, of Isaac, in Genesis 22, has long exerted a spell of fascination over me. I believe it may well be the Hebrew counterpart of the Greek tragedy of Oedipus. But what a different resolution of the crisis! Isaac, unlike Oedipus, is able to take the next step. He is able to transform fate into history.

We all know the story. Upon Isaac rested all of Abraham's hopes of posterity. God promised Abraham a progeny numbered as the stars, but for many years the promise was unfulfilled. At long last was born the son on whom the promise rested. And then — this inexplicable command by God to Abraham, to take his son Isaac and sacrifice him!

If posterity to Abraham is predicated upon Covenant, that is, God's self-revealing bond with man, then this command to sacrifice Isaac would also mean the self-cancellation of God. Obedience to God as the annihilation of God!

Only religious genius of the very highest order could have arrived at such an impossible conundrum. No wonder that Silvano Arieti, in his book *Abraham and the Contemporary Mind* (1981) was led to remark of this story, that "A person raised in the Judeo-Christian tradition always senses in this story the impact of some truth that nevertheless continues to remain elusive."

To continue: father and son wend their way to the altar of sacrifice on Mt. Moriah. Finally Isaac asks, "Behold the fire and the wood, but where is the lamb for the burnt offering?" (Gen.22: 7) Abraham replies, "God will provide himself the lamb for the burnt offering, my son."

The rest of the narrative is carried on in that fateful silence so characteristic of our distant ancestors in their epic moments, i.e., without anxiety or personal feeling. Isaac does not speak again, but the question he has asked —"Where is the lamb for the burnt offering?" — is important. He did not speak on his own behalf. How could he? How could the thought ever occur to him that he is the intended of the sacrifice — he, the beloved son of the promise?

On the contrary: to offer up an animal is only to do what is customary in these situations. Is not custom too a fact of divine dispensation? Isaac's question thus opens up the legitimate claims of tradition and custom and speaks on their behalf.

Thus with Isaac we see how *custom* can help in the support of the *covenant*. Especially is this true if we take Abraham to be — as in Kierkegaard's *Fear and Trembling* — representative of the uttermost radical obedience to the covenant. History is threatened by such radicalism. Mere custom or continuity, on the other hand, can sometimes not be distinguished from stagnation. Radicalism demands too much sacrifice; mere continuity demands too little.

The God who substitutes the ram in place of Isaac is the God who makes the *covenant of generations* — with an offering that can fulfill the claims of both custom and covenant.

I have dwelt at some length upon this story because it seemed to me that the incident mentioned in the previous chapter contains the hint of an Isaac-tale. The reader will recall that General Cocke opposed Mr. Jefferson's intentions with regard to Dr. Thomas Cooper, whose hostility to religious doctrines went against the custom of most Virginians. Cocke's stand evoked strong language — he said, "... if I had expired under the trial I would have held out to the last."

Truly, that is an Isaac speaking! In opposing Mr. Jefferson's radicalism, Cocke helped to avert a certain fate, that of a public university appearing to promote a secular agenda. [1]

General Cocke may not have seen Dr. Cooper's contribution to the book, *Memoirs of Dr. Joseph Priestley* (1806), in which Cooper had written: "The time seems to have arrived, when the separate existence of the human soul, the freedom of the will, and the eternal duration of future punishment, like the doctrines of the Trinity and transubstantiation, may no longer be entitled to public discussion." [2]

Nevertheless, General Cocke knew enough to get the general drift of things. Mr. Jefferson's radicalism had to do with his belief that religion should

---

[1] Cabell made the point that one obnoxious professor might pass muster in a group of appointments but that to commence operation of the University with Cooper alone would be to draw too much attention to his views.

[2] Dumas Malone, *The Sage of Monticello*, Boston, 1981, p. 376.

be a purely private matter.³ To say this is to withdraw the protection of custom from religious expression, and ultimately to break the covenant between the generations. For it is not solely the practice of religion that unites one generation to the next. It is how religion interacts with education, custom, expectations and the formation of character.

The Jeffersonian "wall of separation," while appearing to leave the authority in religious matters up to the individual, in reality deprives religion of the support of custom. The government becomes the umpire or mediator at the religious smorgasbord. The situation then arises, that the citizen is free to practice the religion of his choice, while the government is free to develop itself at variance with the customs of the people. Ironically, the "wall of separation" becomes not that between Church and State, but between the people and their government.

All of this, of course, lies far into the future where General Cocke is concerned. He won this round with Mr. Jefferson, but a more pressing problem awaited him and all of his class. For these planters were, taken as a whole, a generation of Isaacs. They were the "first-borns" of the American Republic, the first post-Revolutionary generation. In a later chapter we will see how this "riddle of the firstborn" applies to General Cocke poignantly in his own life.

But the fate that hung over this "generation of Isaacs" was the problem of slavery and the Union. The chasm between radicalism and continuity continued to widen. With the Civil War America lost its generation of Isaacs at one blow. The inheritors became the outcasts. He who had been Isaac became Ishmael.

ii. Work of Regeneration

"**1843. Dec. 30** In looking back upon my past life, among the few recollections upon which I dwell with ... approbation, is the reception my heart gave to the first announcement of the African Colonization scheme.

First formation of the Society December 1816 — about that time I lost my first wife and in January following [when?] I was under the overwhelming affliction the announcement of the scheme [in the press] was first [made] which diverted my attention from my own misery. I embraced at once without conferring with flesh & blood, what seemed to me to be a heaven-directed measure, and I thank God he has given me grace, to continue my feeble efforts for its support from that moment to the present

---

³ How, then, does a scientist like Dr. Cooper feel himself qualified to attack it? This is a blurring of boundaries. John H. Rice, the Presbyterian clergyman who wrote to Cocke about Cooper, "did not want students to be exposed to a man who disseminated heretical ideas with such intrepidity and displayed liberality only to those who agreed with him." Malone, *The Sage of Monticello*, p. 376.

time. And it is one of the daily objects of my prayers, that he will enable me to do more & more for it to my life's end. But alas!

[1843. Dec 31] How few, even now, sympathize with me in this work . . . This grand Moral & Religious civil & Political enterprise is destined to form an Era in the history of Nations —.It will prove the best means under Providence of removing the curse of slavery from our country while it possesses the high recommendations of bestowing liberty & civilization & Christianity upon injured Africa . . ." [4]

The rich cotton land in Alabama and Mississippi was a boon to the Southern plantation economy in the 1830's. Planters in the Upper South whose lands were exhausted could buy land in the Deep South, bring in surplus slaves to work it, and realize profits.

Or they could merely repeat the cycle of exploitation and ruin, this time to the tune of cotton profits. This dim view of things was no doubt present to the Old General's mind as he toured the Lower South. Cocke was no frontiersman. He was neither fleeing poor harvests nor poor husbandry. On the contrary, he was a good steward. But there was now entered a new consideration to good agricultural practices. Slave emancipation was to be the new goal, the redeemer of cotton profits. What he was after was the soil, the soul, and the Savior.

He had seen it coming — this careless and casual American habit of using up and moving on.[5] In his earlier days Cocke had noted the diminishing fertility of the land in the Tidewater region. He had sold his original estate there to his sister (and later regretted saddling her with an unproductive property, though she said she was glad to have it.) He speculated as to the reasons — intemperance and luxuriousness among the propertied classes, tobacco farming, even the abrogation of the entail. [6]

The creeping waste was afflicting central Virginia too, especially the tobacco crop, which depleted the soil faster than any other. The Albemarle Agricultural Society, founded in 1817, labored to reverse this trend. Cocke, ever vocal and active in this society, was forever engaged in soil-building ventures — marling, manuring, crop rotation, deep ploughing, terracing, ditching, and fencing with hedgerows. Contemporaries called him a "disciple of cow-

---

[4] John Hartwell Cocke, Journal, 1843, University of Virginia.

[5] "By 1845 everybody traveling West . . . understood that the new country was rich in five primary resources – land, minerals, furs, timber, and government subsidy – and that of these, the last was by far the easiest to reach and exploit." Lewis Lapham, *Waiting for the Barbarians*, p. 67.

[6] This is mentioned by Coyner, , p. 154. Coyner also noted that it was the landowners who owned the largest numbers of slaves who were generally the most receptive to the anti-slavery cause. Ironically, the abolition of entail or primogeniture, in which the oldest son inherits the property, disfavored the anti-slavery cause as well as good husbandry.

dung and vegetable excrement," but honored his corn with the epithet "Cocke's Prolific."

But the problem of problems was slavery — the "triple curse." He was visiting Alabama at the time, in 1844, and in one place noted some exhausted and abandoned fields. He writes: *"I could not but ask myself how this could be brought about. The answer is comprised in a single word — slavery. Oh slavery, thou triple curse — a curse to those who suffer the degrading influences of its [...] — a curse to those who [inflict?] the demoralizing [...] by its [...] upon themselves, and a curse upon the country which must . . . suffer all the evils comprehended in a degraded & neglected domestic & Rural economy."* [7]

Perhaps in the use of these words "triple curse," Cocke was recalling the words of his mentor, St. George Tucker, who had compared slavery to original sin. If we do not eradicate it now, Tucker had written, will not our posterity "execrate the memory of those ancestors, who, having it in their power to avert evil, have, like their first parents, entailed a curse upon all future generations?" [8]

Tucker's proposals attempted to balance the interests of abolition with the legitimate rights of property-holders. [9] Cocke must have heeded. In his Journal of 1838 he carefully outlines his plan for emancipation:

"It has been confidently reported that a laborer in the cotton districts in the South... may make $200 clear on an average for years. I believe a large majority of slaveholders in Virginia would readily consent to emancipate their negroes provided they were paid $1000 a piece for their male grown slaves & in proportion to the other & upon receiving in addition ample surety that they should be transported to the Land of their Forefathers in Africa, where they would enjoy the blessings of freedom with a little outfit of means to guard them against the wants & trials of anew settlement on a barbarous shore.

"Now if this be the case, it seems quite clear that five years income from the labor of slaves in Alabama orMississippi would pay the proposed purchase money, and two additional years making seven would be amply sufficient to pay legal interest upon Capital invested. . . my Mind having been long exercised upon this deeply interesting problem, I have determined to visit the Southern & Western states to satisfy myself by [...] & observation as to its practicability – and accordingly left Bremo on the 26th of

---

[7] John Hartwell Cocke, Journal, 1844, Dec. 3. Cocke Papers, Accession 640, Box 188, University of Virginia.

[8] St. George Tucker, *A Dissertation on Slavery : with a Proposal for the Gradual Abolition of It in the State of Virginia*, Philadelphia, 1796, p. 105.

[9] E.g., "In absolving them from the yoke of slavery we must not forget the interests of society." *Dissertation*, p. 104. This is an Isaac-man speaking.

December 1837 for Richmond to make the necessary financial arrangements."[10]

Cocke had already emancipated in 1833 one of his slave families and sent them ahead as his advance guard to Liberia. This was "the gentle Peyton Skipwith," Peyton's wife Lydia, and their six children. "A temperance man and, like so many slaves, a Christian steeped in evangelical faith . . . Peyton seemed to Cocke a fit vessel to carry American genius and the Gospel to Africa."[11]

Once in Africa, Peyton and subsequently his family carried on a correspondence with Cocke and the members of his family. It lasted for thirty years, forming a collection of letters which is "probably the largest and fullest epistolary record left by an American slave family." [12]

Cocke's own letters have not survived. But mingled with the appeals for assistance on the part of the former slaves, there is evidence of affection on their part for the Old General. Peyton writes on September 29, 1844:

> "Dear Master as to myself, I am as well satisfied as I can be in this little Community & I must thank you sir, for the care you had over me while I was young, for when I was young & knew nothing you studied my interest. [13]

From James Skipwith, a nephew to Peyton, in 1859 from Monrovia:

> "I have found that a man must have an Education to be a man in enny cournty I now regret that I did enprove my tallent when I warse young I now see that what you tould me ware for my own Good" [14]

As these passages attest, the Old General received confirmation from his former slaves as to the worth of his educational and evangelical efforts. On one occasion during his travels in Alabama as well, as he writes to his son Cary Charles:

> "I have met here with a very sensible colored Man, who has spent 4 years as a Methodist missionary in Liberia. He has confirmed me in the opinion, that it would be neither justice to the young commonwealth, nor humanity towards individuals to send them there, unless they are to a certain

---

[10] John Hartwell Cocke, Journal, 1838. Signed; the document has the character of a will or testament.

[11] This and quote preceding from *Dear Master : Letters of a Slave Family*, edited by Randall M. Miller, University of Georgia, (1978) 1990, p. 39.

[12] Miller, *op.cit.* p. 11.

[13] Miller, *op.cit.* p. 80.

[14] Miller, *op.cit.* p. 131.

degree intellectually & morally improved far above our common cornfield Negroes." [15]

General Cocke owned a copy of Charles C. Jones' book, *The Religious Instruction of the Negroes in the United States* (Savannah, 1842). [16] Now in the possession of the Special Collections Department at the University of Virginia, the book bears the Old General's signature and an occasional underlining. At the following passage there is a pencilled notation —"They [i.e., the Negroes] nurse us in infancy ... watch around our languishing beds in sickness; share in our misfortunes, weep over us when we die..."

Not only does this passage and Cocke's response to it indicate a responsibility of a religious nature, of the kind that Cocke acknowledged when he wrote, "If Negroes have souls to be saved, how great is the responsibility of the masters?" [17] There may also be a dimension wholly personal. The General lost both of his parents when he was about ten years of age — his father dying first and his mother some months later. In his later recollections the General recalled his early days on the ancestral estate in Surrey County, when his only playmates were the slave children.

For these reasons it is not enough merely to say that General Cocke was a religious man, or even, as Randall Miller puts it, that religion was the "linchpin" of the General's plan for emancipation. [18] There were some Baptists, too, who were religious, but Cocke did not think too highly of them. In an entry in 1843 he noted, "... when will God in his mysterious providence no longer wink at the shameful neglect of the Baptist Church of its colored members?" [19]

Skeat's Etymological Dictionary of the English Language reminds us that *religion* is the opposite of *neglect*. [20] It is not enough, therefore, simply to be religious — a truth that Jefferson was aware of when he said that "It is in our

---

[15] John Hartwell Cocke to Cary Charles Cocke, Feb. 4, 1857. Cocke Papers, Box 152. . On this point also compare Randall Miller: "Furthermore, as Cocke wrote in a September, 1831, letter detailing his arguments, the mass of field hands were so ignorant that they could not even count to twenty. Only the romantic or the callous could delude themselves that such people were fit for freedom." Introduction to *Dear Master*, p. 35.

[16] General Cocke met Charles C. Jones and remarked about him — "He is independent in his circumstances — and can therefore afford to perform his great work without any other reward than [that] which he finds in his own heart. But alas! How few there are who have such a disposition to draw on." JHC Journal, 1848, January; Box 188.

[17] John Hartwell Cocke, Journal, 1850, Dec. 31. Cocke Papers.

[18] "Throughout his letters Cocke revealed his manumission dreams as an entrenched faith in the mutability of man through scriptural revelation and useful employment, a belief that weathered many disappointments in his colonization schemes. The linchpin of his plan, then, was successful religious and moral instruction." Randall Miller, Introduction to *Dear Master*, p. 34.

[19] JHC Journal, 1843, June 11. Cocke Papers.

[20] Before checking this I had always thought that 'religion' was derived from *religare*, to bind. However the etymological dictionary states that, "*religion* and *neglect* are from the same root LEG, which appears also in Gk. *alegein*, to have a care for, to heed."

lives and not in our words that our religion must be read." What matters is the next step: whether this insight leads to a dismissal of religion, or to a further realization of it. Jefferson and Cocke took very different "next steps."

* * *

It is interesting that General Cocke used the term "great work" when speaking of Charles C. Jones' evangelization efforts among the blacks. The "Great Work" in essence is Christian magic — the moral regeneration of human nature which can only be accomplished by the Great Emancipator, Christ himself, and then only through freely-given consent. I do not believe that the Old General used the term 'great work' in this sense, nor do I think of him as some sort of Master or Mage of the Right-hand Path. [21]

Still, the 'Great Work' in presupposes at least two conditions: an 'Indwelling' principle within man whereby he becomes able to attain knowledge from the inside out; and secondly, the principle of mutuality or reciprocity. These both presuppose free consent and conscious understanding. Jesus established this realm of mutuality to be the "Door" between himself and others; those who go not through this 'Door' are "thieves and robbers." (John 10:1)

The 'third term' between freedom and sin is *regeneration* — the 'beneficent magic' — the Great Work. The 'Great Work' involves an understanding of how to work with three terms instead of two. In terms of the present discussion, 'Indwelling' is important, and 'original sin' is important, and neither term must be lost. The work of regeneration is the third term that gives meaning to the other two. "I will do everything I can for him, if he will only do everything he can for himself," said Cocke in reference to an overseer who was giving him a lot of trouble.

The term 'great work' for slave emancipation also appears elsewhere in Cocke's writings. Following the Nat Turner rebellion in Southampton, Virginia, in 1831, the Virginia Legislature held debates on the issue of slavery. The Old General welcomed these debates as a sign that public apathy on the question was being overcome. In a letter to Joseph Carrington Cabell, Cocke comments:

> "But we can't get along in this great   work, with the strait-jacket which our state rights gentlemen have put upon us. —We must have the aid of the genl. government." [22]

---

[21] Knowing what the Old General thought of Swedenborgianism, the nearest thing to occultism in his purview, he would probably turn over in his grave.

[22] JHC to J.C.Cabell, Feb. 14, 1832. Cabell Papers, 38-111, Box 23, University of Virginia.

Strangely enough — or perhaps not so strangely— one of the people leading the states-rights charge in South Carolina is our old nemesis, Dr. Thomas Cooper. Commencing an academic career at South Carolina College in 1820, Cooper became identified with the extreme states-rights cause. He defended slavery and favored nullification. "Valuing union too little because he loved liberty too well, he was one of the first to sow the seeds of secession," wrote Dumas Malone, who sketched his portrait in the *Dictionary of American Biography*.

Whether or not General Cocke knew of Cooper's subsequent career, the "state rights gentlemen" were making the preservation of the union as difficult as the radical abolitionists were. Only to a minor degree does the Old General talk about "rights." As one born in the eighteenth century, he would naturally know something of contract theory and the rights of man. Nevertheless, the following passage from his Journal is interesting because it shows how rights are subordinate to Christian justice, and how, in and of themselves, they can only lead to war:

> "If Negroes are admitted to be human beings with immortal souls, then they must be admitted in a state of nature to have all the rights of man. . . . But to make further argument [un?] necessary, we have only to suppose ourselves in the place of our slaves and they in ours — how would the Anglo-Saxon race, regard the argument, which is drawn from the Bible in favor of servile submission! and if [it?] would claim the right of resistance in such circumstances, how can it be denied to them? Then the right must exist in both parties — and as they are directly conflicting rights, war is the inevitable consequence." [23]

Randall Miller brings out quite clearly that General Cocke saw emancipation as a covenant rather than a right. He describes how Cocke assembled his people at the Hopewell plantation in Alabama on a Sunday morning in March, 1841, and addressed them "for two and one-half hours" on "the high duty to their race and themselves devolving upon them." He disclosed to them the terms of his "emancipation covenant": when they had earned their value, he would free them, provided they adhered to five simple rules. These were: not to leave the plantation without a pass, no strange servants to be received without a pass, no fighting, no provoking language to be used amongst each other, and unconditional submission to the authorities he set over them. The slaves swore upon the Bible to observe these rules, and the General then "dismissed them to enter upon the Experiment." [24]

* * *

---

[23] JHC Journal, 1853, Sept. 7. Cocke Papers, UVa.
[24] Randall Miller, *Dear Master*, 1990, p. 142.

About two months' prior to the commencement of the emancipation experiment in Alabama, General Cocke received a letter from Gerrit Smith, a radical abolitionist in New York. Smith urged Cocke to free his slaves — "I ask you, in the name of uncompromising truth; to emancipate your slaves — even though you be sure, that your worst fears of the consequences be realized. Honor God by such unconditional obedience."[25]

But by this time the General had already formulated his plan. The letter from Gerrit Smith underscores the difference between emancipation as a legal fact and emancipation as a covenant. It was to the idea of emancipation as legal fact that Gerrit Smith urged his friend to give his "unconditional obedience." The General's emancipation covenant was based upon his clear-sighted recognition of the wretched plight of the freed Negro in a society that was prejudicial to him — a problem by no means solved in the North. The check upon "unconditional obedience" was the fact of society and its customs, which would present even to the legally emancipated slave almost insuperable barriers.

The General's goal was Christian liberty, not just legal freedom. Rather, legal freedom would follow upon Christian liberty. The rules of good behavior that Cocke enjoined upon his slaves actually went beyond the five simple rules he laid down in the beginning. There was the matter of sexual fidelity — the sanctity of the marriage tie. Perhaps he did not formulate it as a rule because he expected it to be observed as a custom. Many disappointments awaited him in this regard. As Randall Miller remarks, the Hopewell slaves did not always meet the standards of Victorian morality that General Cocke considered proper. In 1830 Cocke wrote to his son, Cary Charles. Speaking of his efforts to provide education for his slaves, he said:

> *"I am sensible that this bold experiment may be unpopular. But the soldiers of the X have as much need of Moral courage as the Soldiers of Fortune have need of natural courage, and, I trust, I shall be sustained by the Christian part of the community & if this be the case, I shall not change my course for the Worldly-wise, for we have the authority of Scripture, that their wisdom is foolishness with God."* [26]

The recognition of custom was not only the reason why General Cocke could not give his "unconditional obedience" to the idea of legal freedom. It was also important for those to be emancipated. The observance of custom on the part of the slaves was their first step on the road to freedom.

Some thirty years later after the General wrote his "Soldier of the Cross" letter to his son, he was still trudging:

---

[25] Gerrit Smith to John Hartwell Cocke, Dec. 11, 1840. Quoted in Coyner, Dissertation, p. 370.
[26] JHC to C.C. Cocke, Jan. 21, 1830. Cocke Papers, UVa.

"Let the man who undertakes the moral reform of the best of our race prepare to bear a heavy cross; but, in reforming the degraded subjects of our Southern Institution, he may expect a burthen almost too heavy to be bourne — with a host of mortifications and disappointments, that will put his fortitude to the utmost trial. But Christian life is a warfare. And shall soldiers of the Great Captain of Salvation prove less gallant and courageous, than aspirants in fields of blood & carnage for this world's short-lived fame? [27]

iii. An Awakened Act of Neglect

In the beginning of the previous section, the "Work of Regeneration," there is a passage from General Cocke's Journal of 1843 which tells how he became involved with emancipation projects and African colonization following upon the death of his first wife.

It is a remarkable passage in many respects, not the least of which is that it makes no mention of his second wife, Louisa, who died that very year, — on May 10, 1843, at the age of fifty-three.

An omission this telling would seem to support the view of John Hartwell Cocke argued by Jon Leonard Urbach in his Ph.D. Dissertation thesis for Florida State University — *God and Man in the Life of Louisa Maxwell Holmes Cocke: A Search for Piety and Place in the Old South* (1983) — hereafter abbreviated as *Piety*. In this work Urbach argues that Cocke was a tyrannical and heartless patriarch who not only did not love Louisa, but actually ignored and neglected her. In this 600-plus page study of Louisa Cocke through her journals, the Old General does not come off too well.

This view of General Cocke differs in many ways from mine. It also differs from Boyd Coyner's comment on this stormy and quarrelsome second marriage. Throughout it all, Coyner says — in words to this effect — "Cocke remained genuinely devoted to his difficult wife."

Neither of these views, in my opinion, does justice to the spiritual dimension and problem presented by this second marriage. While not exonerating Cocke altogether of coldness and neglect, I hope to show the context in which such actions can be seen as part of a larger struggle to define the nature of "Christian liberty."

Louisa Cocke struggled all her life with the problem of obedience. Urbach never really poses the question of what it must have been like for Cocke to live with a Calvinist flagellant — a flagellant not of the body but the soul. In this "mortification" in which Louisa daily lived, her ever-present thought was that of her own "indwelling corruption" and that of others.

But it is on the matter of conversion that the sharpest difference between Urbach's view and mine becomes apparent. Urbach says that Cocke espoused a "creedless religion of deeds" and that he was

---

[27] John Hartwell Cocke, Journal, Dec. 5, 1852. Cocke Papers.

"...a religious eclectic, sampling all evangelical churches while accepting a kind of personal inspiration close to ultraism. Like many men educated in the generation of the Revolution, Cocke had never undergone an authentic conversion experience, and Louisa experienced her duty's 'great desire' by working for his 'sanctification.'" [28]

But I have argued in this book that Cocke *did* experience an authentic conversion through his first wife and her death. This leads to the question of whether "conversion" means that one has joined a church and embraced a creed, or whether an internal disposition of the mind and soul (called *metanoia* in the New Testament — the change of thinking, or repentance) can be gained through becoming a participant in Christian witness. Is the Church the expression of Christianity in history; or is history itself the stage of the working-out of something Christian? This is one of those questions that sometimes played a part in theological disputes. With General Cocke and his wife it may have played a part in their marital disputes.

On a personal level, Louisa as the second wife faced severe difficulties. Not only did Cocke cherish the memory of his first wife — and Urbach mentions Louisa's resentment that Cocke did not commission a portrait of her, while he kept and cherished a portrait of Ann — it was also the first wife who had shown Cocke the way to Christ. One can only pity Louisa for having to follow in Ann's footsteps. The "second wife syndrome" was doubly difficult for her.

To Louisa, Christianity "outside the Church" is heretical. The overwhelming reality of sin and depravity make strict Church allegiance essential.

One has the feeling that General Cocke and his second wife wrangled frequently over "essentials." The General often refused to accompany Louisa to religious services. Or if he did go, he would often be late; once there, he would sometimes leave early. Sometimes at family worship after Sunday dinner he General would "grieve" her by falling asleep. Worse yet, he would go to *camp meeting revivals* of the Baptists and Methodists, whose emotionalism Louisa considered "noisy" if not "grotesque."

Tears, taunts, threats of Hell — these Louisa worked on General Cocke's children; but, as Urbach points out, such methods hardly seem appropriate in a marital relationship. [29]

Perhaps it was such a "wrangling" over what was essential that led to a journal entry by Louisa like the following:

---

[28] Urbach, *Piety*, p. 141. Urbach does not explain what "ultraism" is. He cites Mathews book, *Religion in the South*, which examines the intensely personal relationship of the believer with God that characterizes the evangelical faith. But whether this is "ultraism" I do not know.

[29] "Louisa brought the Kingdom of God to Bremo, but could not force the children to join it." Urbach, *Piety*, p. 368.

"1825.Mar. 18th. My husband was dissatisfied with me yesterday & this morning spoke to me in so harsh a manner as greatly to wound my feelings & affect my spirits. I could not get over it the whole day . . .

19th. [After a church service] . . . I was still so unhappy at the misunderstanding with my husband, that after prayer & self-examination I determined to go & confess my fault in having so long retained the sense of injury I thought he had done me. This I affected not without some difficulty & afterwards enjoyed a great composure of mind from the sense of having performed my duty. O that the remembrance of this distressing incident might serve to render me very watchful over the deceitfulness of my heart & particularly over that infirmity which leads me to be so resentful of injuries . . ." [30]

The reader needs to imagine closely-written pages and pages of this kind. It is pious and heartfelt, but rarely do we obtain a description of what actually happened. Louisa wakes up one morning "with a depressing sense of my sinfulness" and reflects on "the merits of a crucified Savior." On another occasion she prays for "grace to quicken my diligence in the heavenly race! What is there in the poor perishing objects of time & sense that should thus tempt me to loiter as I do, instead of labouring unremittingly to make my calling & election sure!" [31]

On another occasion she reproaches herself for her "proud and rebellious temper" such as "would render me odious in the sight of God." Translated into practice, Louisa set her soul into unalterable opposition to every form of indulgence — such as the enjoyment of dining, the reading of novels (though Urbach says she did allow members of the family to read novels aloud to her), levity, light-heartedness, cheerful gaiety; card-playing, undue privacy (one must always be watchful for the approach of sin), and even dancing. Urbach credits Louisa for many of General Cocke's moral reforms as well as "the putting of Bremo on full temperance alert." Prior to Louisa, Urbach says, the General had been known to enjoy a whiskey at times.

"Friendship with the world," Louisa declared, "is emnity with God." Early in their courtship, General Cocke accused her of trying "to reduce her heart to order by the ascendancy of her religion." [32]

It may be true that the General and Louisa brought out the worst in each other. They argued constantly. Cocke would rebuke her, — one of his "schoolings" — and Louisa would be reduced to tears or nurse resentments.

---

[30] Diary of Louisa Maxwell Holmes Cocke, Book II, Mar.9, 1825—July, 1826, Cocke Papers, University of Virginia.

[31] This and quote previous from Louisa Cocke's Diary, 1825, Oct. 26, Cocke Papers, University of Virginia.

[32] Urbach, *Piety*, p. 65.

According to Urbach, Cocke "usually dismissed [Louisa's] stabbing attempts at intimacy with sovereign disregard."[33]

Indeed so — or he would betray such attempts. On one occasion before their marriage General Cocke showed one of Louisa's [love] letters to his children. Louisa was deeply hurt by what to her was a betrayal of intimacy.

Continuing with Urbach's summary: General Cocke was "too blunt and business-like" to be entrusted with Louisa's feelings. Louisa came to understand that delicacy in feelings meant less to General Cocke than "deference." Says Urbach, "... everyday [Louisa] endured obvious instances of Cocke's disrespect rather than stretching the lines of tension between them still tighter."[34]

Urbach emphasizes that the relationship of General Cocke to his second wife was the relationship of a superior to an inferior. He thus softens the contours of her religious obsession by appeals to feminism: "Not much more than a slave herself, Louisa was the perfect representative of Bremo's slave culture."[35]

It is a sad tale, this second marriage — on the part of the General an awakened act of neglect, on the part of Louisa a prolonged hurt. An *awakened* act, that is, normal human consciousness, — "For I do not the good I want, but the evil I do not want is what I do." (Romans 7:19)

The General was gone from home so frequently that to Urbach he merited the term "absentee husband." Sometimes he would not write, or not write often. On one occasion Urbach did think that the General was "punishing" Louisa by his silence. [36]

Aside from whatever temperamental incompatibility stood in their way, I believe that at a deeper level a fundamental difference existed between Cocke and his second wife in the matter of Christian outlook. Louisa's path was the path of absolute negation — the "willingness to be nothing if it seems good to Thee." [37] Her God demanded prostration — absolute submission. "Lord have mercy on a poor, helpless worm," she cried to her journal on April 26, 1843 — her last entry. Louisa's Calvinism seems submissive to the point of fatalism: "Life is a tale that is already told," she declared in 1827. Or again: "Evil

---

[33] Urbach, *Piety*, p. 146.

[34] Urbach, *Piety*, p. 148, p. 168.

[35] Urbach, *Piety*, p. 449.

[36] This seems far-fetched, in that Urbach links Cocke's not writing in 1841 with an incident that occurred in 1834. In 1834 Cocke hired a minister to do missionary outreach among the Bremo slaves. Louisa was delighted with S.B.S. Bissell and his "animating prayers." Cocke dismissed Bissell eight months later; he thought his preaching too "finished" for his audience. In the meantime, Louisa had committed some "indiscretion" with Bissell, the nature of which is never fully explained. Urbach's discussion of this "indiscretion" takes place in the context of Louisa's possible attractions to other men. In any case, a marked decline set in between Cocke and Louisa from this point. While in Alabama in 1841, Cocke wrote some letters to his children, from one of which Louisa was led to conclude that "he is deeply and forever incensed."

[37] Urbach, *Piety*, p. 565.

man must learn to wait God's 'good time and pleasure' before ascending the pit and escaping the labyrinth," Louisa wrote. [38]

Louisa's idea of Heaven was the realm of "the perfect morning star of perpetual day..." where God's shimmering angels fly to embrace her; where in the crystal "pure atmosphere" she would "know the joyful sound" of angel's harps and where her mind would be prepared to receive Heaven's "music and other pleasures."

What part theology played in fostering this cloying view of the future state, and what part may be attributed to Louisa's fantasies of escape from misery, is difficult to say. But the Gospel "outside the Church" has always resisted this emphasis on submission and personal salvation to the exclusion of all else. General Cocke, the "solitary horseman," often away, could not help but to resist it also. Louisa, lonely in the "moral desert" of Bremo, felt herself forsaken.

But what looks to be heartlessness in one sphere may be spiritual necessity in another. Never more than in this unhappy second marriage does General Cocke seem to stand upon the grounds of the inner freedom of the Gospel — resisting, albeit negatively, Louisa's Christianity — which seemed to have no place for inner freedom. One might have wished he had done it better. One might also have wished Louisa could have followed him there.

"He never gave her love." Thus Urbach on General Cocke with respect to Louisa. I acknowledge that in this second marriage a less flattering aspect of Cocke's character does come to light. But — "He never gave her love"? To me this phrase more truly describes Louisa's God.

---

[38] Urbach, *Piety*, p. 233.

V. Fruit of the Vine

When General Cocke married Louisa Maxwell Holmes in 1821, his six children ranged in ages from eighteen to five. The eldest, John Jr., was 18. He was followed by Louisiana, 15; Philip St. George, 12; Nan, 10; Cary Charles, 7; and Sally, 5.

John, the first-born, was already aware of being a disappointment to his father. For this reason, Urbach says, he reached out to Louisa and tried to bond with her. Louisa, though sometimes declining his invitations to take walks together, assiduously worked for his conversion and was gratified when, in 1831, John took communion and pledged his soul to God. There was backsliding soon after, however. But backsliding was not the sole reason for Louisa's troubles with John. In her Diary of 1826 she makes the first mention of John's "attack." This, says Urbach, is the first recorded incident of John's epilepsy. For Louisa's first five years at Bremo, John was occasionally "forgetful" and "irritable" but otherwise their relationship was stable.

Louisa was shocked by John's convulsion in 1826. She began working diligently toward his conversion. She prodded, nagged, admonished. Urbach reports that she would reproach him for eating too much, would warn him against travelling or leaving Bremo lest an attack come on. On one such occasion after Louisa's naggings John became "restless" and "fretful" and rebuked her for finding fault with him.

Louisiana, the eldest daughter and Louisa's favorite among Cocke's children, died in December, 1829. At the family memorial service for her two months later, John had a violent convulsion lasting half an hour. He had to be hustled out of the room; the family, greatly upset, resumed the service.

As time passed Louisa became John's caretaker. She had to plan meals around his attacks, hide him from company when she sensed a fit coming on, and watch him constantly around fires, ponds, ditches, holes, and culverts — of which at Bremo there are many. It was unpredictable. One moment John would be in his right mind — "at least that portion of it that remains," Louisa remarked — and the next he might be "stretched in the yard in a fit."[1]

Louisa sensed a worsening of John's condition in 1836, when he was in his thirty-third year. He would become "wildly violent," and fall into "violent convulsions", writhing in "agonies of dissolution." On May 16, 1836, according to Urbach, who quotes passages from Louisa:

> "He was sometimes 'quite out of his mind' telling Louisa that 'God was asking him questions continually,'" and 'talking incessantly about going to Heaven,' 'singing downstairs in a wild way,' as Louisa hid upstairs and bursting into her room to tell her 'he knew what *truth* was.'" [2]

Urbach notes that Louisa began to connect John's spells of derangement with Cocke's absences. Barely at equilibrium with Cocke at Bremo, John would become "unhinged" without him. It was as if John needed his father's presence in order to maintain his fragile ego-consciousness.

Once when Cocke rode out on a spring day in 1838, John became "perfectly deranged." Urbach quotes Louisa's account:

> "…His mind took the most extraordinary turn on the subject of salt, which he said was a component part of the idea of sensation, and which he needed to restore his memory and every other function. Under this idea he ate so much as to create sickness of the stomach and then had it put in cold water and put his feet into it. He then ordered cold water to be poured upon his head and finally a quantity of ice to be brought…Through all this terrific scene I was dreading every moment lest he should become perfectly frantic and do some mischief to some of us…" [3]

In this passage Louisa has put aside all of her preoccupations of self-feeling and religion. She achieves a rare faithfulness to the event and a mode of exact description. She was able to become, for John, the "salt of the earth." Helping to stabilize John, she was able to heighten her own faculties of awareness. [4]

Yet another affliction of a first-born awaited Louisa. In 1831, at age nineteen, Nan (Ann Blaws) married Nathaniel Francis Cabell (known as Frank). Nan and Frank became converts to the Swedenborg Church. Louisa accused Frank of atheism; Nan stood by her husband; angry exchanges ensued, with Louisa continuing to point out the error of their ways, sending tracts, and otherwise making herself a nuisance. In 1833 their son and General Cocke's

---

[1] Urbach, *Piety*, p. 385.
[2] *ibid*, p. 385.
[3] Louisa Cocke Diary, May 23, 1838; quoted by Urbach in *Piety*, p. 386-87.
[4] John's cry for "salt" is suggestive. Salt intensifies the forces of consciousness/cognition, the pole opposite from vitality and life. For this reason, people who suffer from heart trouble are put on a low-salt diet.

first grandson, Hartwell, was born. The child was a delight to his grandparents, and Louisa adored him. At three years of age little Hartwell, or Harty they called him, began to have recurrent attacks — the first may have been while he was sitting on his grandfather's lap. It was the same year, 1836, that John Jr.'s epilepsy worsened. Harty seemed to be headed toward the same fate.

Louisa believed that the affliction of Nan and Frank's child was an act of divine retribution, due to their "guilty departure from the simplicity of the Gospel."[5] To Nan and Frank, Louisa finally became unbearable. They turned to Cocke, who complied with them from that point on by insisting to Louisa that he monitor all of her letters to the Cabells. Indeed, the Cabells never forgave Louisa for blaming their religious practice for Harty's afflictions. During Louisa's final days, they were the only family members not in attendance.

"Surely it is a trying case that the two first borns in the family should be so afflicted," wrote Louisa on July 10, 1836. [6]

It is somehow poignant that Louisa, absorbed in her own domestic drama with General Cocke, was also called upon to play a part in the "Afflictions of the first-borns." With John, she acquitted herself well; with Harty and the Cabells, perhaps less well. In her destiny she indeed becomes something of Hagar in the "moral desert" she considered Bremo to be. "And as she sat over against him, the child lifted up his voice, and wept." (Gen.21:16)

Louisa and General Cocke had no children. Louisa is thus not one of my "Foremothers," and yet a gesture of hers had a part to play in making possible my existence.

Louisa was not fond of Cocke's second son, Philip St. George, whom she considered "amiable but not very bright." She found in him "a want of moral courage." He was "dull, restless, unconverted, his goals unfocussed, his ideals unfixed." [7]

After Philip's graduation from West Point, Louisa gave herself permission to indulge in a little "strategem" that led to the shy Philip's courtship of his future wife, Courtney Bowdoin. I do not know what the little 'strategem' was, but had it not been carried out, I would not be here to write this book. Philip St. George Cocke was my grandmother's grandfather. The lines of inheritance seem as tenuous sometimes as the threads spun by the Fates.

*　*　*

In 1816, the young General Cocke was planning a vineyard. [8] But that is about the last we hear of it. In 1828 the General took the pledge of temper-

---

[5] Urbach, *Piety*, p. 390.

[6] *ibid*, p. 392.

[7] *ibid*, p. 328.

[8] See Boyd Coyner, "John Hartwell Cocke: Southern Original," in *The Bulletin of the Fluvanna County Historical Society*, No. 6, June 1968.

ance and forever after his emancipatory and evangelical efforts are intertwined with his temperance crusade.

It is this aspect of Cocke's character which, more than any other, fails to win the sympathy of later generations. It went against the grain of his contemporaries too. An old toast of the Fluvanna County taverns, relished by the family as well as reported by Coyner, went something like this — "Here's to the great state of Fluvanna. May she be delivered from the sheep-sorrel and the Timberlakes, from the Hessian fly and John Hartwell Cocke, and by God's help old 'Flu' will come through all right."

In his journals the Old General sometimes struggles to reconcile his temperance views with Christian communion service. In 1859 he notes that at the institution of the Last Supper, Christ uses the term *fruit of the vine*. Acknowledging this, General Cocke goes on to say that unfermented and unintoxicating juice is equally *the fruit of the vine* as is fermented and intoxicating wine.

We may think that the Old General is indulging in a bit of sophistry here. But we have no cause for feelings of complacency when we consider how, in modern society, so many of our intellectual addictions have become institutionalized. In many ways we could do with a temperance crusade in the field of intellectual endeavor. Much in the Old General's life recalls an "old general" way of thinking. In some important respects he is closer to Isaac in the Old Testament than to us. This is true particularly in his attitude toward posterity and in matters relating to moral self-government, spiritual discipline, and obedience.

General Cocke was very much aware of the partial nature of his efforts for slave emancipation. He hoped that his children or later posterity would carry on with the work that he began —

> *"Oh Lord, I ask not for my children or their descendants —the honors & wealth of this world... but make them thy servants ... make them content with their condition ... and raise up among them some (if they are not all now so disposed) who will be faithful executors of my will in regard to my Alabama scheme — and Bless, oh Lord, this Essay to do some good in my day and generation — not only to the intended recipients of the boon, but to those who labor in the bestowment of it ....* [9]

It was a hope not to be realized — not in his children and, once the Civil War broke out, not in his own life. Nevertheless, the ideal which General Cocke expresses in this passage is that of the faithful steward, a role to be maintained through the generations. Like the chivalric ideal which inspired the stories of the Knights of the Grail, it fused the spiritual ideal of stewardship with hereditary obligation. It is a generational task, and in the passage above, Cocke

---

[9] John Hartwell Cocke, Journal, Nov. 5, 1844 — Apr. 11, 1845, Cocke Papers, Box 188, UVa.

expresses the hope that his children and descendants will be up to it. It is most striking that in this passage Cocke eschews the notion of "honors and rewards in the world" for a deeper concept of family honor.

It is interesting that the theme of racial tolerance played a part in the stories of the Holy Grail. Parsifal, one of the best-known of these Grail knights, had a half-brother who was the son of his father and a black maiden, a Muslim. In Wolfram von Eschenbach's version (ca. 1210) of the Grail legends, this half-brother of Parsifal, Fierefiz by name, comes to the Grail Castle and accepts baptism in order to marry a Grail maiden. As he dips his head into the baptismal font, which is placed before the Grail, a writing appears on the Cup for all to read: "If any member of the Grail Company should, by grace of God, be given mastery over a foreign folk, he must not speak to them of his race or his name, and must see to it that they gain their rights." [10]

For the essential component in General Cocke's concept of family honor was the "bestowal of a boon" — seeing that the slaves attained the honorable state of liberty. The idea of *bestowal* – so radically different from the modern fad for "self-esteem" — is important to the concept of honor. Bertram Wyatt-Brown, in his study of the Percy family, quotes a seventeenth-century Spanish play about honor by Lope de Vega, in which a character exclaims, "Honor is that which is contained in another; no man grants honor to himself; rather, he receives it from others." [11]

I believe this view of honor is a more truthful rendering than that expressed, for example, by Drew Faust, when she characterized the Southern code of honor as a way of maintaining power. Speaking of the symbolism of dueling, she remarks that "... the power of South Carolina's master class depended to a great extent on symbols and display... A symbolism of violence made clear to all how quickly selective force would be invoked to reinforce the structure of power." [12] This interpretation seems crudely reductionistic.

Honor is the mutual recognition of transcendent human possibility. The code of honor indicated a willingness to fight (as with the duel) or to sacrifice oneself in the labor to bestow a boon, as Cocke put it. That displays of honor could go to absurd lengths — in Faust's example, two students fought a duel over a dish of trout — does not mean that violence was being used to maintain power. Rather, it indicates that the supreme principle of non-utilitarianism, of transcendent possibility, even self-sacrifice, must be continually renewed.

"A covenant, not a right." General Cocke's stewardship was based on fatherhood as a spiritual ideal. Indeed in his old age, as the Civil War raged, "the

---

[10] John Matthews, *The Grail: Quest for the Eternal*, London, Thames & Hudson, 1981, p. 29.

[11] Bertram Wyatt-Brown, *The House of Percy*, Oxford University Press, 1994, p. 9.

[12] Drew Gilpin Faust, *John Henry Hammond: A Design for Mastery,* Louisiana State University Press, 1982, p. 18. Incidentally, John Henry Hammond 'decried the idea of a federal subsidy for slave emancipation.' (p. 47)

idea of an Abrahamic Covenant intrigued the General's mind, and was an intellectual key in his shifting beliefs." [13] Coyner finds in the General's "shifting beliefs" a pilgrimage from Thomas Jefferson to George Fitzhugh — from the "rights of man" to proslavery advocate. Coyner writes, quoting in part from General Cocke:

> "Bondsmen were committed to their masters as a religious responsibility. When in God's good time the masters were all converted, *"God will make Slavery — a part & parcel of the only [true] & reliable Conservative principle of free republican Government."* Then would all men be ready *"to receive the Miracle as the basis of the Uni[versal] Emancipation of fallen Man."* Evidently the slave would have to wait for the Second Coming!" [14]

Rather than "a pilgrimage from Jefferson to Fitzhugh," — if anything, I have argued that General Cocke was not exactly a Jeffersonian — the thoughts of the General's old age were a continuation of, rather than a break with, the same idea that informed his lifelong efforts at slave emancipation. In his old age, however, the idea of the Abrahamic covenant came to the foreground. In this respect he shares much with the defenders of slavery, who used the idea of the Abrahamic Covenant to urge reform and amelioration of the slaves' condition.

It is true that in his very last writings the General seemed to seek Biblical justification for slavery. George Fitzhugh did this in his *Cannibals All,* which is an indictment of Northern "wage-slavery." But there is, I think, a difference in the approaches of General Cocke and George Fitzhugh. For Fitzhugh the Biblical justification was an end in itself. With Cocke I have the feeling that he was looking *through* the Biblical argument for a covenantal idea that would be workable in America.

What is a covenant? It is an agreement, a promise, an expression of mutuality. It is usually connected with matters of high expectation and importance. It is doubtful, for example, that I would make a covenant with a friend to meet for lunch, though if my life depended on it I might. When God made his covenant with Abraham he promised, "I will make of thee a great nation." (Gen.12: 1-4) In the Old Testament there is forever the expectation of covenant and the chastising of the people when they fall away from it. When they are unable to maintain the high degree of consciousness necessary for divining God's will, they succumb to legalism or self-pity, like Esau who lost his birthright: "Behold, I am at the point to die; and what profit shall this birthright do to me?" (Gen. 25:32)

The birthright, the continuation of the covenant, demands an intuitive consciousness attuned to the "being-ness" of the world. For the world is full

---

[13] Coyner: Dissertation, p. 565.

[14] Coyner: Dissertation, p. 568.

of things; but behind all things are the Beings. Mortal man is caught in an intellectual consciousness that perceives the things; another step in consciousness is necessary to perceive the Beings. The making of the covenant is a ceremonial act of making this other step in consciousness. It signifies the emancipation of the human soul from its bondage to things, to mortality. Indeed, what use would such a covenant be to a man who only feels himself about to die? The covenant emancipates man into participation with the Being of the world.

With covenant man bonds his words to the real world, the world of Beings. He does this by honoring his words. No one can be emancipated *from* the world. By keeping the covenant one is emancipated *into the world* by means of one's words. Honor brings the world of the covenant along with us. The same distinction holds with the problem of slavery. Emancipation as a covenant has to do with the fullness of personality — of possibility, of "inheriting the earth." It is a question of bringing another soul into its rightful patrimony. It is a supernatural relation, a matter of honor between two parties. But emancipation as a legal right is more a question of power. The struggle between *inheriting the earth* or *gaining power* becomes an important one in the twentieth-century continuation of the struggle of blacks for full emancipation.

VI. A Covenant, Not a Right

The feminine counterpart of "patrimony" is *matrimony*. Counterpart — but not equivalent. The two words have very different meanings, but together they form an important part of that "old general way of thinking," which, as far as some aspects of modern America are concerned, may as well belong to the Stone Age. There were certainly people in General Cocke's time who thought so too, and in many respects they helped to form the world we know today. Their ideas define to a large extent what we mean by the words "modern," or "modernism." Extremely influential, yes — but it is a testament to the power of that "old general way of thinking" that we characterize these ideas as "modern," thus distinguishing them from that reservoir of vague feeling which is all that remains of that "old general way of thinking."

On July 5, 1826, when Louisa Cocke on her 38th birthday was recalling her fifteen years of Christian commitment and reproaching herself for her "proud and rebellious temper," she would have been shocked and offended to know of an incident that occurred on the previous day.

On July 4, 1826, the English reformer Robert Owen (1771-1858) delivered his "Declaration of Mental Independence" in the town square of his intentional community in New Harmony, Indiana. Owen argued that in 1776 men had fought not solely for political liberty. They fought for the right to think freely "on all subjects, secular and religious; and the right to express those thoughts openly." [1] Robert Owen appointed himself as the standard-bearer of this new charge, which was to make war against the three evils of society that had corrupted and confused human beings — namely, religion, private property, and marriage.

---

[1] Quoted in Celia Morris Eckhardt, *Fanny Wright: Rebel in America*, Cambridge, Harvard University Press, 1984, p. 129. This book hereafter cited as Eckhardt, *Wright*.

It was a decisive moment for Frances Wright, who was one of Robert Owen's devoted admirers. Fanny, born September 6, 1795, orphaned at a young age, was an independently-wealthy Scotswoman then living in America. She had visited America a few years previously, and her book, *Views of Society and Manners in America* (1820) was laudatory — some thought excessively so. She was an admirer of Jefferson and Lafayette.

The day Robert Owen delivered his new "Declaration" was significant — both Jefferson and John Adams, the third and second presidents respectively, died on this day, fifty years after the signing of the Declaration of Independence. For people like Fanny Wright, the future belonged to Robert Owen who, she said, was to "influence the condition of mankind [more] than any individual that has ever existed." [2]

At that time Frances Wright was planning her own intentional community, and she was very impressed with Robert Owen's ideas on communal living and co-operative labor. But where Owen labored in the leavings of German immigrants (he had purchased the village of Harmonie, Indiana, from some followers of George Rapp; these industrious and religiously-bonded souls had increased by ten times the original worth of the village and surrounding farms) Fanny intended to found a community among slaves, to be dedicated to the worthy purpose of their emancipation.

It might have worked — this little commune in Nashoba, Tennessee. There was some initial resemblance to General Cocke's plan, in that it would require the slaves to work out their purchase price. But here the resemblance ends. There was no idea of religion or covenant to form a context for the gaining of freedom by the slaves. James Madison, in fact, though supporting Fanny's efforts, noted that Fanny's project offered no substitute for religion, which had made the Harmonist and Shaker communities so successful. [3]

Some years back, after the publication of her *Views of Society and Manners in America,* General Lafayette had written an appreciative letter to Fanny. He invited her to visit him, and Fanny accepted; she ended up staying three years with him and his family at La Grange, his estate outside of Paris.

General Lafayette [1757-1834], also born on September 6 — though of course much older — became a sort of soul-mate and father-figure to Fanny. W.E. Woodward, one of Lafayette's biographers, remarked that Frances and Lafayette had not so much a love affair as a father-daughter relationship. Frances at one time asked Lafayette to adopt her. She accompanied Lafayette

---

[2] Eckhardt, *Wright*, p. 130.

[3] Eckhardt, *Wright*, p. 111.

[4] To "lafayette" someone means to "load him with honors." When Lafayette visited America this "Friend of the Revolution" was treated like a Grand Potentate. America indulged its forbidden fantasy for royalty in a year-long orgy of banquets, toasts, ovations, speech-makings, dinners, ceremonies, awards, band-playings, town-namings, ribbon-cuttings, and parades. Lafayette loved every minute of it. According to the banker, Lafitte, he was "a statue in search of a pedestal"; to Jefferson, Lafayette had a "canine appetite for fame."

in 1824 during his famous "Grand Progress" through America. [4] Or rather: not quite "travelled with" but, in Fawn Brodie's words, Fanny travelled with Lafayette "at a discreet distance." Together Fanny and Lafayette visited Mr. Jefferson at Monticello. [5] It was at that time, according to Fawn Brodie, that Lafayette expressed to Jefferson his opposition to slavery, and his belief that slaves should be freed and educated. Jefferson agreed to this only in part — "he was in favor of teaching the slaves to read print; that to teach them to write would enable them to forge papers, when they could no longer be kept in subjugation."[6]

Brodie remarks that both Lafayette and Frances Wright were attempting at this time to "prod Jefferson out of his apathy about Negro education and emancipation."

After her visit with Mr. Jefferson, Frances wrote a letter to him soliciting his support for her intentional community. Jefferson replied though at age eighty-two "I do not permit myself to take part in any new enterprises," still "that which you propose is well worthy of trial."

Jefferson did not live to see the failure of the Nashoba venture, nor read of its denunciations in the press. In an article on Fanny Wright, O. B. Emerson details the influences upon her that led to the formation of her community. [7]

Fanny gained insights, and in some cases material assistance from, James Monroe, James Madison, John Marshall, and Benjamin Lundy, who was prominent in the anti-slavery cause. Lafayette himself had attempted a slave emancipation project on his plantation in French Guiana, a project halted by the French Revolution.

But what actually happened, Emerson remarks, was that "[Frances] took her stand against the institution of marriage — a stand that was to contribute to the failure of her future activities for social reform."[8]

This disciple of Jefferson was like him in failing to take account of custom and covenant. But she carried her opposition a step further than he did by including within her condemnation the institution of marriage.

Robert Dale Owen [1801-1877] son of the reformer, described Fanny as "conservative in manner and language," but "radical in politics, morals, and religion." In later life he regretted the influence that Fanny had had upon him, and commented, "[She had] ideas on many subjects, social and religious, even more extravagant and immature than my own."[9]

---

[5] General Cocke led the brigade that welcomed General Lafayette at Yorktown and accompanied him to Charlottesville. Urbach mentions Louisa Cocke's meeting with Lafayette in the context of her possible attractions to other men. On October 19, 1824, Louisa attested to the "warm feeling" she received after "a cordial shake by the hand" from Lafayette. Urbach, *Piety*, , p. 186.

[6] Fawn Brodie, *Thomas Jefferson: An Intimate History*, New York, 1974, p. 462.

[7] O.B. Emerson, "Frances Wright and Her Nashoba Experiment," *Tennessee Historical Quarterly*, December, 1947, 291-314.

[8] Emerson, *op.cit.*, p. 294.

[9] Emerson, *op.cit.*, p. 301.

In 1827 some reports of life at Nashoba were published in Lundy's periodical, *The Genius of Universal Emancipation*. Fanny was in Europe at the time; the reports were those of James Richardson, a trustee of Nashoba who was in charge of publicity and correspondence. Some portions of these reports shocked the world:

"Dilly having given utterance a day or two ago, to some grumbling at having so many mistresses James Richardson stated to them ... that the multiplicity of superiors ... is of palpable advantage to them ...

"... Isabel had laid a complaint against Redrick, for coming during the night of Wednesday to her bedroom, uninvited, and endeavoring, without her consent, to take liberties with her person. Our views on the sexual relation had been repeatedly given to the slaves; Camilla Wright [Fanny's sister] again stated it, and informed the slaves that, as the conduct of Redrick, which he did not deny, was a gross infringement of that view, a repetition of such conduct, by him, or by any other of the men, ought in her opinion, to be punished by flogging. She repeated that the proper basis of the sexual intercourse to be the unconstrained and unrestrained choice of *both parties*.

"Nelly, having requested a lock for the door of the room in which she and Isabel sleep, with the view of preventing the future uninvited entrance of any man, the lock was refused, as being, in its proposed use, inconsistent with the doctrine just explained ...

"Met the slaves — James Richardson informed them that, last night, Mam'selle Josephine [one of the slave girls] and he began to live together; and he took this occasion of repeating to them our views on color, and on the sexual relation..." [10]

The world was horrified by these reports — the refusal of a lock on the door, and the public cohabitation of one of the trustees with a slave girl. One reader wrote: "What is this but the creation of one great brothel?"

Richardson in reply defended cohabitation of the races, which he said was going on in the South anyway, though it was kept hushed up. He concluded by saying, "I am an Atheist, and on the diffusion of Atheism rests my only hope of the progress of Universal Emancipation." [11]

Fanny Wright, learning of these developments at a distance, responded on January 26, 1828, with a long article in the Memphis *Advocate and Western District Intelligencer* in which she re-affirmed her purpose to raise the Negroes

---

[10] Emerson, *op.cit.*, p. 305-307.

[11] This and preceding from Emerson, *op.cit.*, p. 308.

up to the level of the whites and then amalgamate the races. She attacked the institution of marriage and made her own "Declaration of Moral Independence," to which she dedicated Nashoba as the place "where her principles would be carried into practice." [12]

Frances remained unalterably opposed to marriage for some time. But by 1830 it had become apparent that her experiment in slave emancipation had failed. In company with a gentleman, she transported her 31 slaves to Haiti, where they were freed. This gentleman, with the piquant name of Phiquepal d'Arusmont, Fanny married. She was thirty-six years of age. The next twenty or so years of her life were passed, according to Celia Eckhardt, with respect to her married life, in "tight-lipped privacy." It was not a happy union. The couple later separated and there was a bitterly-contested divorce.

Fanny's daughter by this marriage, Frances Sylvia, or Sylva, who had been mainly raised by her father, later became an ardent Christian. She once said that the moral of her mother's life was that "the present woman's movement is tempting my sex to man's province to the neglect of its home duties and joys."[13] In 1874 Sylvia testified before a Congressional Committee against female suffrage.

Sylvia and her mother remained permanently estranged, Sylvia even refusing to see her mother during her last illness in 1852. Despite these sorrows, Frances Wright became a sort of feminist icon for women in the nineteenth century and on into the twentieth. It says a great deal about the woman's movement that it should rally around this early disciple of collectivism. "No human being can be, or ought to count for, more than a unit in the great, collective sum of civilized power," Fanny had written. It was not even a maxim that she herself had lived by. The great social reformer and rebel ended up singing hymns to the commonplace, the conformist, and the petty.

* * *

Thomas Jefferson, Frances Wright, General Cocke: these individuals dealt with the issue of slave emancipation in very different ways. Those different ways depended, more than any other single factor, upon the presence or absence of religion — the idea of covenant.

Does the covenant idea inform the twentieth-century struggle for black civil rights? If so, what metamorphosis can we see in it? These questions become our leading focus as we turn to the more contemporary setting of this study. The transformations of the idea of covenant can be seen in the events in Birmingham.

---

[12] Emerson, *op.cit.*, p. 309.
[13] Eckhardt, *Wright*, p. 290.

Interlude: Some Vignettes

It is a hot night in July, 1963, and I am fifteen. My father has brought me with him to a meeting at the courthouse in Birmingham, Alabama. The meeting was called by people desirous of keeping the schools open in the face of a recent court decree ordering that some desegregation take place this coming fall.

My father and I sit upstairs in the gallery. Down on the floor, amid loud boos, hisses, catcalls, a frail schoolmistress is speaking in favor of keeping the schools open. In favor of complying with the federal desegregation order.

I hear a scuffling and a whispering behind me. I glance back to see a very fat man with crutches and an open-necked shirt gesturing to a comrade. Handing his friend one of his crutches, the fat man instructs his underling to "go beat up that bitch" after the meeting is over. But there are so many interruptions, catcalls, threats, shouts and disruptions that sheriff's deputies are soon called in to disperse the crowd. I do not know if the schoolmistress who spoke got away safely. The meeting had lasted barely an hour.

My father later wrote: "This adds up to the fact that a tremendous amount of missionary work in the community needs to be done in the face of these court orders which, of course, must be complied with." In later years I wondered if that fat man was J.B. Stoner, a notorious Klansman who was active in many of the bombings around Birmingham. There was a lot of unrest in the city in those days, and the possibility of violence was never far from our thoughts.

* * *

It is the afternoon of December 30, 1972, and I am on a visit home to Birmingham from Boston, where I was then living. My father and mother are there; my brother Tom has driven over from Atlanta with his wife and family. His old school friend and drinking companion, Steve, also shows up that afternoon. Steve is currently studying for the ministry at the Episcopal Theological Seminary in Cambridge; he comes wearing his collar.

Someone offers Steve a drink; he declines it. He says he has joined Alcoholics Anonymous. There is dead silence in the room. My parents are drinking heavily in those days. The conversation invariably gets around to religion, which is a sore subject with my father. Tom brought up the matter of what to do about his children's religious education. Steve said he would not have the children baptized unless the parents had some general sympathy with the principles of the Christian religion. My father says he wants to get away from "supernaturalism and all that stuff," though he does admit that he holds to the "ethical principles" of Christianity. Tom began to talk about archetypes and about how necessary it was to have an understanding of the symbolism. My father says again what he has said many times before, that he wants his body donated to the Medical Center when he dies. He says science can explain what we do not know. Tom had been talking about feeling wonder when he looked up at the stars, and said:, "I'm glad you believe in science, P.J." (Our father, Paul Johnston, insisted that we children call him 'P.J.') P.J. said he believed in the

Unitarian Church. Tom said: "This is what Unitarians are like: they believe in science and know all the answers by claiming not to know the answers." Mother got a bit aggressive when she demanded of Steve to know "what God was." Steve had gotten around to the Protestant Reformation, and that knowing and believing in God's existence are two different things, and that the God he believed in was the Creator; when P.J. launched into recitations from philosophy about the ontological proof of God, etc. He was trying to prevent Mother from talking so much, although he was talking a great deal himself. Steve, sensing a blind alley, changed the subject.

* * *

It's sometime in the early sixties. I am in a car driving from Montgomery to Birmingham with a young man, a Harvard student, who has come to Alabama to help in the civil-rights struggle. He is older than I am, intelligent, educated, committed. He is talking about the struggle, about his commitment to social justice, about how bad things are down here, about how Clifford Durr is the only white lawyer in Montgomery who takes civil-rights cases. I listen to him go on and on; I look out the window at the soft green landscape, red clay, meadows, pine trees. I finally say something about loving Alabama in spite of all its problems.
"What do you mean?" he asks. "It's the land," I say. "I love the land."
"I don't understand," he says. "What do you mean, about loving the land?"

* * *

Again, it's early sixties. Our family has gone down to the L&N train station to fetch my brother Paul, who is returning home from Vanderbilt, where he is at college. The L&N station, unlike the other train station in town, the Terminal Station, was built in the heydey of the segregation ordinances. That is, the L&N station was even more segregated than the Terminal Station. In the L&N station, they segregated even the ticket counter. A row of plastic potted plants divides black and white.

My father enters the L&N station on the black side; a few heads are raised. He sees the row of plastic potted plants and charges into them like the proverbial bull at a red flag. The planters shatter on the floor; the ticket agents rear up in alarm and threaten to call the police. My father shouts that this is intolerable, he won't stand for it, it's a travesty. Amidst the dumped-over divider and spilled fake dirt and a few other choice epithets and curses my father makes a quick exit, the ticket agents scurrying to clean up the mess.

My father used to have a phrase about "joining the human race." I believe in this expression he found an idea of covenant that made sense for him. He thought people who hadn't made the decision to join the human race were arrogant, psychologically unbalanced — on the way to neurosis. It seemed to make some sense at the time — this gradual merging of the concepts of human mutuality and dignity into therapeutic liberalism. Many white Southern liberals were making a similar accommodation — simplifying religion to health or politics. It seemed to harmonize with the messages then sounding from the leaders of the black civil rights movement, where the pure springs of religion were bubbling up from what seemed to be metaphysical depths. It was a fountain not tapped since the days of Luther or Moses — or so some of its spokesmen — bearing some of these same names — said.

In later days Martin Luther King expressed exasperation with some of these white liberals. By then liberalism had become the risk-free guarantee of the saved.[14] My father failed to take into account what happens when a doctrine becomes respectable. For the liberals, too, found a way to join causes without having to first take out membership in the human race. And when the blow came they left him forsaken.

Here is where the covenant of liberalism breaks down. It is hard to be both alone and forsaken.

---

[14] One of Birmingham's "limousine liberals" once remarked that in the days of the black civil rights movement, all you had to do — i.e., as a white person — was to "show up."

Rowe Lawyer Loses Post in Birmingham

By JOHN HERBERS
Special to The New York Times

BIRMINGHAM, Ala., May 29 — An attorney's decision to represent a Government undercover agent in the Ku Klux Klan has cost him his membership in one of Birmingham's most prominent and affluent law firms, reliable sources said today.

Paul Johnston, who took the case at the indirect request of Attorney General Nicholas deB. Katzenbach, confirmed in a telephone interview that he was leaving the firm of Cabiness & Johnston and would establish his own office in Birmingham within a few days.

Mr. Johnston said that any statement about the reason for his leaving would have to come

THE NEW YORK TIMES, SUNDAY, MAY 30, 1965.

Attorney for Rowe Loses Post in Firm

Continued From Page 1, Col. 4

from a spokesman for the firm. His brother, Joseph T. Johnston, the firm's managing partner, said the incident was a "purely internal" matter and that there was "no need to go into the reason."

"There is no story in it," he said.

It was learned, however, that the firm had objected to Mr. Johnston's taking the case and that his decision to do so anyway had been responsible for his departure.

Another lawyer who is not in the firm said it was "a very delicate situation that involved family differences." Mr. Johnston's father, Forney Johnston, also is a member of the firm.

A few days ago, Mr. Johnston agreed to defend Gary Thomas Rowe Jr. in a law suit filed by Matt H. Murphy Jr. of Birmingham, chief lawyer for the Klan. Mr. Rowe was the Government's star witness earlier this month in the murder trial of a klansman.

Mr. Murphy sued Mr. Rowe for $6,000 in legal fees that Mr. Murphy said had accumulated before it was learned that Mr. Rowe was an informer for the Federal Bureau of Investigation. It was on information sup-

plied by Mr. Rowe that the Government arrested three Klansmen and Mr. Rowe in the murder near Selma, Ala., of Mrs. Viola Gregg Liuzzo, a civil rights worker from Detroit. Mr. Rowe testified in the trial of one of the defendants in Hayneville, Ala., earlier this month that he had seen two of the defendants shoot into the car that Mr. Liuzzo was driving.

Mr. Rowe, who had been an undercover agent for the F.B.I. for several years, was unable to provide his own defense in the suit filed by Mr. Murphy.

Mr. Katzenbach asked Bernard G. Segal of Philadelphia, co-chairman of a lawyers committee for the defense of civil rights cases, to find a private attorney licensed in Alabama to take the case. Mr. Segal then contacted Mr. Johnston.

Cabiness & Johnston is one of the oldest law firms in Birmingham and has some of the most lucrative accounts in Alabama. It has 10 or 11 partners, including the three Johnstons, and eight or nine associates.

The firm is not known to have handled any cases involving civil rights. Paul Johnston, however, has differed from the other members of the firm on social issues. He is a member of the Southern Regional Council, an Atlanta-based organization concerned with equal rights for all.

Mr. Johnston has also been active in civic work in Birmingham and in 1962 he was elected Birmingham's "Man of the Year" by a panel of local leaders.

Firm Ban Taking Care

Mr. Johnston said he agreed to take the Rowe case on the request of Mr. Rowe and on the recommendation of Mr. Segal. Another lawyer, however, said the firm had met on the matter and had "on an overwhelming vote decided that no member would take the case."

The decision for Mr. Johnston to leave the firm apparently was made at a meeting of the partners yesterday.

"His decision to take the case was in keeping with the high standards of ethics in the legal profession," a lawyer said of Mr. Johnston, "If anything it would have enhanced the prestige of the firm to take it."

The lawyer added, however, "it is not too popular here to be involved in such matters."

Most Birmingham lawyers have avoided civil rights cases. There have been at least two other instances in which lawyers who took civil rights cases later separated from their partners.

<u>New York Times</u> article on Paul Johnston, May 30, 1965

VII. The Magic City

They called it the Magic City because it grew so fast. In 1883, when Joseph Forney Johnston moved there, it had only 3,000 inhabitants. In another forty years it would become the third-largest metropolis in the South, and in another forty would acquire more somber epithets — "the most segregated city in America," the "City of Fear," "Bombingham."

In the summer of 1947, few months before I was born, the first dynamitings occurred. They decreased for a time in the early 1950's; but then rose again after the 1954 *Brown vs. Board of Education* declaring the "separate but equal" doctrine unconstitutional. They continued for many years thereafter. Birmingham was a violent place in my youth because there was only one issue of any real importance that was being decided, and that was "Integration." The struggle was writ large in black and white. It was about how the two races were going to adjust their memories of each other to a common citizenship, and whether the two histories could become one.

Some people in the early days of the civil rights movement referred to the movement for black civil rights, more gingerly, as "Desegregation." Maybe this seemed to them a less loaded term. But as I begin this journey through the remembered past I am going to stick with "Integration" because this word resonates beyond the social and political field. For "Integration" is both spiritual and personal. If I learned anything from my young years, I learned that "Integration" is very difficult to achieve. The conflict between the black and white races was the open, public and historical event. Privately, internally, I was trying to achieve my own "integration." And so were the people around me.

Internal integration sometimes intersected at the public events; at other times it seemed to run another course, quite removed from public happenings. It was all very complex. It is not enough simply to look at what someone thinks, or to look at what happens to him (his history) or even to his memory

— what he says he remembers. All three of these strands have a part to play in the complexity — that complexity being the effort, on the part of any human being, to achieve a measure of integration. For people often believe contradictory things. They have contradictory thoughts; their thoughts and beliefs are sometimes at odds with each other.

For example: my father was a liberal, a Unitarian, a disbeliever in Christian supernaturalism, a believer in racial equality. At least, these were the things he professed. These beliefs made up his public *persona*, his mask, the self he revealed to the world. He hated Birmingham, hated the South — or at least, he said he did. He wanted nothing to do with Bremo (built by slave labor, although he acknowledged that his great-great grandfather General Cocke was a humanitarian.) For my father, the trinity of the good was: Harvard, Unitarianism, and liberalism. Yet, strangely, after Harvard and his wartime experiences, he returned to Birmingham to practice law in a family firm that had been founded by his own father, to whom he was not close. Then he married a Southern Patriot (my mother). And then he had to watch as two of his children — my brother and I — grew up to be conservative.

These are some of the strands of contradiction woven into his history. At the moment I want to pursue a small contradiction in my father's nature. Whenever he would speak of his paternal grandfather, Joseph Forney Johnston, the governor of Alabama from 1898 to 1902, and later a Senator, a twinkle would come into his eye. This happened only one or two times; it was a small thing. Yet I want to know why there was this mood of warm and humorous remembrance when my father recollected his grandfather, recalling how his grandfather would sit on his porch with his pony of bourbon — that is, a slug of bourbon in a shot-glass — and tell his stories. And when P.J. related such times to us, he became, for that moment, not the Fighter for Social Justice, but simply, a man — a man with a story to tell, a story that was one link in a chain of stories.

Such "integrated moments" — that is, moments when I felt I really knew my father — were, as I have said, rare. For the grandfather, as for the grandson, race was the problem that loomed at the meeting of the three roads. W.E.B. DuBois, who founded the N.A.A.C.P., believed that the "color line" was the central problem of America. It was "The Riddle of the Sphinx" — the riddle of race. It was the "soul-waking cry" that came, not from the East, nor from the West, but from the "sad, black South."[1]

* * *

"The sad, black South" — maybe old Grandfather Johnston had something to do with that, though in his day he fought Yankees, and later, carpetbaggers, not Negroes. My great-grandfather was in high school when the Civil

---

[1] W.E.B. DuBois, "The Riddle of the Sphinx," in *The Burden of Race: A Documentary History of Negro-White Relations in America*, ed. Gilbert Osofsky, New York, 1967, 224-5.

War broke out. He enlisted in the war, eventually receiving four wounds, one of them serious. In the battle under Jubal Early's command near Winchester, Virginia, a shell pierced his lower ribs. He fell from his horse, and, gaining consciousness later that night, was able to work it out of his body, stanching the flow of blood with his handkerchief. He recovered, eventually landing in Selma, Alabama, where he began to practice law. "He delighted to drive the spear of question through the armored mail of doubt" [2] — and he doubted the law. He moved to Birmingham and switched to banking.

It was the Reconstruction era. "We saw not only our financial ruin, but saw we had lost our liberties . . . We reread our parole and saw that this cruel, unnecessary penalty was not written in the pact made for us between Grant and Lee at Appomatox. We rebelled and entered upon a war against reconstruction. It was in this just cause that Joseph F. Johnston enlisted as a political warrior and led the citizens [of Alabama] to victory, and with them unfurled the banner of white supremacy..."[3]

Mr. J. Thomas Heflin, a colleague in the House, put it in even more graphic terms:

> "...he was a terror to the vandal horde that came into Alabama to incite the negroes and to plunder our people, and no one did more than he to protect our women from the lust and carnality of the brutes in our midst and to drive out the scalawags and carpetbaggers and to give back home rule..." [4]

Captain Johnston was elected governor of Alabama "to unite the white voters of the State," as the *Dictionary of American Biography* puts it. There is some ambiguity in the matter of race, however, for he later lost favor with the Democrats in his second term "because of his equivocation over the issue of a constitutional amendment to exclude blacks from state politics." [5]

In other words, the exclusion of blacks was a step Governor Johnston was unwilling to take. My father also sensed some "equivocation" on the matter of race with respect to his grandfather. In a shipment of Johnston family papers to the Alabama State Department of Archives and History, he wrote to the state archivist about "two items of interest," one of which was the following:

---

[2] John H. Bankhead, in *Memorial Addresses on the Life and Character of Joseph Forney Johnston*, Washington, D. C. , 1915, p. 18 .(Hereafter cited as *Addresses*.)
[3] Francis S. White, *Addresses*, 57-58.
[4] J. Thomas Heflin, *Addresses*, 84.
[5] Special issue, *Journal of the Birmingham Historical Society*, November, 1982, Vol. 7, Nos. 3 & 4: "Town Within a City: The Five Points South Neighborhood, 1880-1930;" p. 18.

" 'Race Antagonism' (JFJ) This is an undated, handwritten, unsigned, 18-page paper, so titled, written in the handwriting of Joseph F. Johnston, the Senator and Governor. It is evidently an attempt on the part of J.F.J. to organize his thoughts and reach some level of mental comfort in coming to grips with the overriding problem of the day …This essay is fragile and difficult to read and in skimming through it I gather he resolved the matter by recourse to the traditional Southern conventional wisdom, namely, the low state of the Negro in Southern culture is due to his inherent moral and intellectual inferiority to the white man. I have the feeling that this paper yielded him very little mental comfort."[6]

In any case, the people (at least the ones who voted) loved Johnston enough to elect him to the governorship and later to the Senate, in which he was glad to serve, he said, "to aid the Government that my forefathers helped to establish."

People believe contradictory things. Senator Johnston may have been pleased to serve in the Senate, and to aid the government his forefathers helped to establish. But he was also proud of the four wounds he received during the Civil War. In his brief sketch of himself that he wrote for the Congressional Directory, he confined himself to a bare recitation, without embellishment, of the facts. "Only once is there the appearance of even claiming any superiority over anyone, and that consists in the recital of the fact that as a Confederate soldier 'he was wounded four times.'"[7] He wanted his friends to know that he regarded those four wounds on behalf of a lost cause as a badge of honor.

The old Senator had reason to resonate with lost causes. Joseph Forney Johnston was a descendant of Gilbert Johnston, who fought on the side of Bonnie Prince Charlie. The battle of Culloden, in April, 1746, put an end to the dream of restoring the Stuarts to the British throne. It was a slaughter lasting forty minutes — "Some 1,000 of the Young Pretender's army of 5,000 weak and starving Highlanders were killed by the 9,000 Redcoats, who lost only 50 men," says the *Encyclopedia Britannica*. Bonnie Prince Charlie, whose subsequent destiny may have been an inspiration for the portrait of Mr. Toad in *The Wind in the Willows,* after hiding out for some months, finally escaped to France disguised as a sewing woman. He died in 1788, "sodden with drink and disillusionment."

As a result of the Battle of Culloden, Scotland went through its own reconstruction era. British statutes eroded the powers of clan chieftans, banned the wearing of kilts and tartans, and confiscated arms. But the lure of economics proved superior to British might. *Brittanica*: "Indeed, the gradual paci-

---

[6] Letter, Paul Johnston to Mimi Jones, August 13, 1982.
[7] Address of Mr. Williams of Mississippi, in *Memorial Addresses,* p. 49-50.

fication of Scotland and its partial integration into a united Britain probably owed more to a growing prosperity than to legal changes."[8]

After the defeat at Culloden, Gilbert Johnston fled to North Carolina. His great-grandson, Senator Johnston, was a beloved, genial old man who used to enjoy his slug of bourbon on the porch and tell his tales of Lee and Early in Virginia and Bonnie Prince Charlie at Culloden — remembered wars fading into familial ones, and all of them lost causes.

The Senator died in 1913 while in office in Washington. Shortly thereafter, his two grandsons, Joe and Paul, aged about eight and six, walked around the Senator's old neighborhood in Birmingham, distributing his calling cards to friends and acquaintances. It was a prank the old man might have appreciated, though the parents of Joe and Paul did not.

That neighborhood, the "Nabob Hill" section of Five Points South in Birmingham, is where — in my memory — I am standing now. It's in the early 60's, it's an early September day, it's early in the morning, and Ramsey High School is about to be integrated. In 1927 the houses along "Nabob Hill" were demolished to make room for this high school. In its earlier incarnation it was the scene of my father's earliest years. And it is now where my father and I have come, to be a part of the throng of anxious spectators. My father is standing next to me, his brow furrowed, his look preoccupied and worried. There are police cars everywhere, walkie-talkies, news cameras, a lot of tension. There is an early-fall feeling to the air, a few reddish-brown leaves curled on the sidewalks. Everybody is hoping there won't be trouble. We are all waiting for the black students to arrive.

My father's liberal views on the race issue were regarded, in Birmingham, as a betrayal of his position and class. These views attracted the attention of Northern liberals, however, and in 1965 the then Attorney-General, Nicholas DeBrian. Katzenbach, asked him to represent an unpopular client.

In those days the state of Alabama had acquired a bad reputation for violence. One of those acts of violence was the slaying, by some members of the Ku Klux Klan, of Mrs. Viola Gregg Liuzzo, a civil-rights worker from Detroit. This slaying had been witnessed by Gary Thomas Rowe, a former nightclub bouncer and undercover FBI agent who infiltrated the Klan.[9] In a parallel move which had no direct bearing on this case but which, in the climate of the time, was too close for comfort, the lawyer for the Ku Klux Klan, Matt Murphy, brought suit against Gary Thomas Rowe in order to recover a sum

---

[8] "I think you're being too nice to the Brits. Perhaps the prime reason that Scotland was integrated (that word again) into England is that the English went up into the highlands in the decades after Culloden & simply killed off the most powerful highland families and clans. Nowadays we call it 'ethnic cleansing.'" Editorial note, Paul C. Johnston, October 29, 1995.

[9] Rowe's autobiography, *My Undercover Years with the Ku Klux Klan* (Bantam Books, 1976), is not considered reliable by historians. Now out of print, it was popular in its day. Paul Johnston receives brief mention in it.

of money which he claimed Rowe owed him. The Justice Department of the United States asked Paul Johnston to represent Rowe in this suit.

This case exploded like dynamite in our lives. In agreeing to take the case, Paul Johnston went against the expressed wishes of his firm. Defending the ethical imperative of the lawyer to represent unpopular clients, he cited the professional principles of the American Bar Association, in which "law should be so practiced that the lawyer remains free to make up his own mind how he will vote, what causes he will support, what economic and political philosophy he will espouse." He also made reference to an acceptance of retainer for legal services by John Adams, 175 years previous, of eight hated British soldiers, a request refused by most members of the Boston Bar.

But arguments in favor of autonomy of conscience, whatever their derivation, did not carry weight with the firm. My father's employment with the firm was duly terminated. As an afterthought, and after further consultation with a friend, my father wrote a second letter to the firm acknowledging their right to refuse any litigated matter for any reason.

But it was too late; the damage had been done. The story was front-page news in the major newspapers of the time. I was away at boarding school at the time, and read the story "Attorney for Rowe Loses Post in Firm," on the front page of *The New York Times* for Sunday, May 30, 1965. I felt very far away indeed, up in a corner in New England, while all these events were going on. It was the complexity again — so far removed from the severe New England simplicities — and this time it was exploding.

Another newspaper, *The Washington Post*, editorialized: "The darkness in Alabama seems to have grown very deep." A member of the firm was quoted as saying that, "We thought it was a matter that was out of bounds for a firm of our kind." The *Post* noted the contrast, that of a large corporate firm and the case of a "comparatively impecunious individual" like Rowe, unable to obtain legal counsel in a minor civil action. It quoted Paul Johnston, the ousted lawyer, who said simply: "No lawyer who has any feelings of responsibility could turn down a request like this. You can't live alone in these times."

But the impecuniousness of Rowe was not the reason the firm interdicted the case, and it was interesting that the *Post* brought it up as a possible explanation for the firm's refusal. In those days anything having to do with civil rights and racial tensions had far more to do with passion than with money. Liberals in Alabama would often point this out. They would point to Atlanta — growing, flourishing, commercial Atlanta, Birmingham's rival — as a place where passion was held in check by self-interest. [10]

---

[10] In heeding to its self-interest, Atlanta was like a Yankee city. David J. Garrow in his biography of Martin Luther King confirms this, when he recounts how the president of Atlanta's Chamber of Commerce met with business leaders. They all thought the race issue was tarnishing the city's image, and wanted the matter resolved. "Get us off the hook," they said, "even if it means desegregating the stores." David J. Garrow, *Bearing the Cross*, New York, 1988, p. 151.

To which in reply one critical wit rejoined, from T.S. Eliot: "The last temptation is the greatest treason/ To do the right deed for the wrong reason." The poet's perception seemed finer and more apt than the worldly and sterile reasonings of the journalists.

Paul Johnston, 1937

In time, of course, Birmingham would come to terms with the race issue, a chastened newcomer to the national pursuit of self-interest. But that time lay still in the future. After the catastrophe, letters of support and appreciation to my father poured in from all over the country, many of them bearing the promise of future business. Leon Jaworski wrote him that, "There may be hurts and reprisals as a result of your responding to the call of duty, but in the end you will find your unselfish and courageous act will bring you the respect of your fellow citizens." Judge Skelly Wright wrote, "I am proud to know you," and Anthony Lewis, then of the London Bureau of *The New York Times* wrote "to let you know that you have admirers in England as well as all over the United States."

The goodwill was there, even if it was beamed from points distant from Birmingham. But the future business never materialized. Ten years later, on February 11, 1975, I received a letter from my father in which he confessed—

> "The underemployment which has characterized my situation for the past several years, when my law practice began to dry up with no prospects for betterment in the future, has not been easy to take. The work ethic is too deeply imbedded in my character for me to maintain psychological equilibrium in the absence of a reasonable amount of intellectual fodder to chew on. Age is not on my side but I keep sustained by the hope and belief that extrication from the cage I'm in can somehow be accomplished in the not too distant future."

By that time, Paul Johnston's legal practice had sunk to a smattering of small business and social security cases. The case itself fizzled: Matt Murphy, the Klan lawyer, was killed a few months later in an automobile accident. What had consumed my father's professional life dwindled to nothing, ashes in the end.

* * *

In 1977 I received a letter from my mother:

"Again, we loved your letter — I feel that we have a great deal of strength — Your father has it sometimes & in some ways —   not in   others. I am not saying this for you to think that I am more religious, or ... a stronger person —   but deep down ... I feel I am a much stronger emotional person than Daddy. — Darling, everyone has to believe in something. — Sometimes I fear Daddy does not have a deep belief in life after death — his is in human beings — intellectual and on the scientific side... This is difficult to express also."

My mother, Isabelle Berry Johnston, followed my father into Unitarianism. But her religious feelings could not be contained in the narrow-necked bottle of the Religion of Reason. They overflowed into Nature, flower-arranging, children, gardens, and for a while, prize chickens. And finally they overflowed into the habit of the cocktail. As the years went by she practiced, less and less, the Bach partitas, the Chopin études, the Mozart sonatas, that she had perfected in earlier days. The music burst out of her at times, a trill, a cadenza, a few bars of a fugue — like sudden crazes, erratic remembrances, collected resolutions, to do better, to begin again: not to forget.

My mother came from Rome, Georgia, and I loved visiting my grandmother Berry and cousins who lived there. My grandmother Berry, whom I called "Dearma," and I had a warm companionship. We played endless games of Canasta, watched "Secret Storm" and the other soap operas on T.V., we went grocery shopping together. Still, Dearma was something of an enigma to me, especially about the race issue. Aaron worked for her, a soft-spoken, light-skinned, gentlemanly Negro who lived nearby with his family. He would wear blue overalls, in which was perched, in an upper pocket, a red can of "Prince Albert" tobacco. I would watch, fascinated, while he rolled a cigarette with one hand.

One morning, when my mother and I were visiting Dearma, I wandered down the road to Aaron's house and became happily involved in playing with Aaron's children. Some while later, my mother appeared, with an anxious demeanor. She said that I must come back to Dearma's house, that Dearma had been upset to learn that I was playing at Aaron's house. My mother's anxiety was not on her own account, but on account of Dearma. Isabelle attributed her mother's racial fears and anxieties to the fact that she was from Detroit. Dearma was uneasy and reserved around black people, in fact she was reserved with people in general. My mother, who as a child had once refused to act the part of the "North Wind," attributed her own easygoing, friendly personality, and especially her ability to get along with black people, to her "Southernness."

My mother, something of a Southern Patriot, was rather an odd companion to my father, given his Yankee-loving ways. My father was dismissive of his Southern past, but it returned to him in the form of marriage. Isabelle's husband, like her mother, was ill-at-ease with the fluidity of Southern character. It was Isabelle who learned to pick up the pieces, smooth the jagged edges, keep things going. The marriage could not have been an easy one. My mother never really recovered from the deaths of two of her children: the firstborn son Forney, whom I never knew, and little Isabelle, the twin sister of my youngest brother John. She grieved alongside a man who took his emotions stoically, by the drop; and by the 1960's even these emotions were directed largely toward social causes.

My visits to Rome provided a welcome interlude from the humorless and self-defining nature of these social causes. The Berrys were fun. They liked horses and dogs, fishing, hunting, boating, swimming, water-skiing. When I visited Dearma, in the days of late childhood, I would sleep in the room next to hers. It was more like a porch than a room, with enormous windows opening out into the night. With the moon shining behind the branches of the oak trees, and the sound of a train in the distance, I knew, even then, that I could wish for no greater joy.

* * *

Throw a stone into a pond. Can you notice how the rings eddy as a group from the center of impact which has, in the meantime, become smoothed out again?

The event in my life that was like that stone thrown into water was the 1954 *Brown vs. Board of Education* decision declaring the "separate but equal" doctrine unconstitutional. Yet looking at that event directly is like looking at the place where the stone broke through the surface of the water. The surface has cleared, the center surrounded; the event has been absorbed into the texture.

The repercussions were for me the eddying waves that mark the boundaries of childhood. I was seven years old in 1954, a pupil in Miss May Ward's School, too young to know much of the great world. Miss May Ward had also taught my father before me, some forty years ago, and probably much in the same way. She taught the five elementary grades in one room, one grade to a row. We younger children had the benefit of hearing the older ones recite their lessons. I remember the fireplace in the schoolroom, the old wooden desks, playing "Red Light, Green Light" on the narrow sidewalk along Miss May Ward's house at recess.

All of this changed when I was placed in public school for third grade. I came not knowing how to tell time, a fact embarrassingly publicized to the class one day by my teacher. Still, I am grateful; the memory of this embarrassment forever marked in my mind the difference between time and pre-time, between the timeless and the historical.

My father wrote a letter to *The Birmingham News* in the wake of the *Brown* decision, declaring his support for the then-budding civil-rights movement. Born in 1908, he was then about forty-six years of age. I have mentioned before the idea of the "moon node," the eighteen-year rhythm in biography. My father experienced his second moon node, his 37th year, in 1945, an important nodal point indeed for mankind in general. [11]

During the Second World War, Paul Johnston served in the Navy as a lieutenant in the legal corps. After the war, he was one among the fleet of lawyers on Justice Jackson's staff at the Nuremberg Trials. The published transcripts of these trials, *Nazi Conspiracy and Aggression*, later took up a prominent corner on his bookshelves. He often recounted to us children his memory of interviewing Hermann Goering in his jail cell — Goering, one of the masterminds of the Nazi movement, who later committed suicide in his cell with a capsule of cyanide that he had secreted in his anus. Goering, remarked our father, understood English perfectly but insisted on German translation in order to gain time to frame his replies.

My father's experience in postwar Germany may have led to his contracting of tuberculosis. On the voyage back home he began coughing blood, and for the next few years he was in and out of sanitoriums. It was during one of these confinements, at Saranac Lake, New York, that he encountered an old-fashioned bearded psychoanalyst of the Freudian school. He underwent analysis, and in six months was cured of his tuberculosis. This was before the age of penicillin. Never did my father waver from his conviction that the analysis had been the means of working his cure. From that time on he was a convinced Freudian, and in time the works of Freud began to take up a prominent place in his bookshelves as well.

These three events — the Nuremberg Trials, tuberculosis, and psychoanalysis — were constellating events in my father's life. They were the points of reference, the initiating events of his entrance into the Modern Age. There was little in his career up to then — Miss May Ward's School in Birmingham, St. Albans' in Washington, the Hill School in Pennsylvania, Harvard, and finally Yale Law School — to suggest the social rebel, humanitarian, or freethinker.

My father's support of the civil-rights movement placed him in opposition to the society we knew, whose maxim, like that of most societies everywhere, is that it is easier to get along by paddling with the current. Yet on Thursday and Sunday evenings my parents and we children dined at the Mountain Brook Club, where white-coated waiters swooped back and forth bearing drinks and supper dishes. [12]

---

[11] John Lukacs called 1945 "the year zero." The bomb and the era of the two world wars that it closed seemed to mark a radical break from a not-too-distant past that contained so many hopes for progress and enlightenment.

[12] Walker Percy mentions this Mountain Brook Club in one of his books, I think it is *The Last Gentleman*. He mentions the clicking shoes of the golfers who swarmed in and out of the dining

"Miss Clara," 1925

The succession of drinks began to tear at the social interactions; the family fabric frayed from one end to the other. At one end there was alcohol dependency; at the other end there was moral conviction and thought. It seemed as if irreconcilable forces were eating their way from opposite ends toward the center. At the center there were the disastrous financial schemes involving our parents and our oldest brother. My brother Paul often spoke of this time. It stamped him with melancholy and anger of intellect, to remember how the wealth that had taken generations to acquire was dissipated by our parents in a decade and a half. For a time Paul connected this dissipation with the loss of religion. Our side of the family had abandoned the religion of the ancestors, and he thought that the confusion we were experiencing was a kind of retribution for this apostasy.

In the 1970's Paul began an exploration of Christianity, and in his "Spiritual Autobiography" he wrote:

> "I noted that one of my ancestors was an elder of Unity Presbyterian Church, a detail I discovered only a few years ago. When I did so, I immediately thought of the line from *All the King's Men* spoken by Willie Stark: 'I was a Presbyterian when it still had some theology in it.' I'm willing to bet that the Presbyterianism of my ancestors, like Willie Stark's, had plenty of theology in it. But not enough, or maybe too much, because it turns out that one of my line — Joseph Forney Johnston, the soldier and successful politician — abandoned the religion of his Scottish forebears to become an Episcopalian, and in fact even had a hand in the

---

room on golfing afternoons. Reading this gave rise to one of those shared historic recognitions : he, too, was there. Later the surface of this clickable floor was changed to conventional carpet, and in some ineffable way the robust character of this dining room was forever changed to dull-suburban.

establishing of St. Mary's Episcopal Church on Highland Avenue in Birmingham... Because of him, decades later, my earliest church memories are of Episcopal services and Sunday schools, but whatever the reasons he might have had for making this change, I can say that his attempt to graft Anglicanism onto our line never took. At least, I never saw his son and grandson — that is to say, my grandfather and father — in an Episcopal Church."

The "Spiritual Autobiography" goes on to describe our grandfather, Forney Johnston, who became the husband of Clara Cocke:

"My grandfather, whatever he might have been nominally, remained a dour, hard-working, hard-judging, tight-lipped Scottish Calvinist to the core of his being, perhaps even more rigid than his Presbyterian ancestors because, unlike them, he was never in a religious community capable of channeling or tempering his stern outlook. He came to hate most of what happened from the New Deal onward, made good money fighting New Deal legislation, some of it all the way to the Supreme Court, and in his old age retired to his wife's plantation in Virginia and to as close a proximity to the Old South as money could buy, which in Fluvanna County Virginia in the 1950's was pretty close."

Finally the "Spiritual Autobiography" comes to our father:

"My father, as probably had to be the case, given the domineering, unrelenting character of my grandfather, was a rebel, but never a clear-eyed one. After World War II, and while trying to recover from tuberculosis probably contracted in Germany, my father went into psychoanalysis — from which he emerged hating his father and just about everything his father stood for. The experience must have been beneficial. My father immediately got well; but then, strangely, he returned to Birmingham, rejoined the family law firm, and managed to be both courageous and confused, both competent and incompetent, as well as drunk-just-about-every-night, for the better part of a decade and a half. When he was fired from the family firm for various liberal stands in the 1960's, he sadly let the competent and courageous side fall away — leaving only the other."

My father loved Harvard; his reunions there and with his Fly Club cronies were intellectual vacations from Birmingham. With his love for Harvard and Freud, it was no wonder that when the young, Harvard-educated and psychoanalytically-trained doctor, Robert Coles, came to Birmingham to deliver a talk at the Unitarian Church in the early 1960's, P.J. went up to him and struck up a friendship. In fact my father bore Robert Coles back to our house as a kind of prize. It was mutual. A few years later a fictionalized Paul Johnston appeared in the portrait of Dr. James Butler in the work that made Robert Coles famous — his *Children of Crisis* (1964).

In a letter after that talk, Robert Coles spoke of the happy accident of a friendship that came out of "that little confused talk over [at] the Unitarian Church... It goes to show that planning and calculation have to bow to blessed fate." At this time Coles was studying children in newly-desegregated schools under the auspices of the Southern Regional Council. In 1971 he wrote to me, saying that he "sent the second and third volumes of *Children of Crisis* to them [i.e., my parents] and I gather from what your mother wrote to us that your father is struggling through all the sadness that those volumes unfortunately have to possess."

Indeed there was an undercurrent of sadness in those years. The decline that began with the Rowe business set in with a downward spiral of alcoholism, *laissez-faire* childrearing, and disastrous financial machinations involving my oldest brother, who was determined to redeem the family by making millions. The sadness spoken of by Robert Coles was thus not entirely a sadness over the plight of the people of Coles' concerns: the poor, the migrant workers, the factory hands, of America. But in his refusal to avert his gaze from "man's inhumanity to man," Paul Johnston was very much of his time — of that period in the 1960's when the country as a whole seemed to share these concerns.

"The riddle of the sphinx" — my father was asked this riddle, and he answered it with his belief in racial equality. It was his unwavering faith — unwavering at least for the time that he acted as a citizen in the public sphere and became the "Man of the Year." But as time passed I saw how he became, in his later years, a disbeliever in his own history. He would resist the efforts, by some, to make him into a sort of hero of the civil-rights era. In later years he seemed hardly to want to talk about his efforts on behalf of black civil rights. He was devastated when, in the 1970's, some Harvard professors published studies summarizing the poor performance of some black children on some I.Q. tests. "My life's work is in ruins," he said to me. "Everything I have stood for, everything I have fought for." And he made a gesture of resignation, of giving up.

His answer to the Sphinx: was this finally the reason for his choked silence? There were many things he did not want to talk about as the abyss of the "year zero" widened in his own soul. The abyss into which he did not want to look became the past about which he did not want to speak.

Top: Virginia and Clifford Durr with Michael Hamlyn, an English visitor, September, 1963;
Bottom Left: Caryl, about 1967;
Right, brother Paul C. Johnston, 1963.

Statue of Vulcan overlooking Birmingham's Southside

"Suddenly and very sadly it seemed to me that I had strangely come in Birmingham to the other side of something remembered."

Jonathan Daniels, *A Southerner Discovers the South*

VIII. The Other Side of Something Remembered

i. Tribal Loyalty

When in 1954 a letter in support of the *Brown vs. Board of Education* decision appeared in *The Birmingham News* with Paul Johnston's name on it, Virginia Foster Durr in Montgomery went to the telephone and made a long-distance call to Birmingham. She welcomed Paul into the fold of white Southerners fighting on behalf of racial equality. She was also renewing an old acquaintance from her Birmingham years, long ago when all the best people lived on the Southside, around the Highlands Country Club and Niazuma Avenue. Virginia Foster grew up there. Her family suffered a decline in fortune when her father, a minister, was expelled from the Presbyterian Church because he refused to teach the literal truth of Jonah and the whale. Despite their difficulties, the Fosters were connected with those people who were, in my grandmother Clara's words, "the fine families," or "the people from the best families."

As a young girl, Virginia looked up to Clara Johnston and modeled herself on her, considering her the epitome of the Southern Lady. The friendship continued after the Johnstons moved to Washington, D. C. in the 1920's, when Mr. Forney was representing the Southern Railway. Joe and Paul attended St. Alban's. Virginia was attending the National Cathedral School, and one spring vacation, not having sufficient funds to return to Birmingham, she stayed with the Forney Johnstons.

But after those early days, a breach developed in the friendship. Virginia tells the story of her journey into Liberalism in her autobiography, *Outside the Magic Circle* (1985) which, characteristically, is told in the form of a long reconstructed conversation. I say "characteristically" because Virginia Durr was the most gifted conversationalist of my acquaintance. When I was growing up in Birmingham, I made many trips to Montgomery to see her — or rather, to hear her. She was "... a real spellbinder... whose peculiar charm lay in her enormous curiosity about people, her driving passion to find out things, to know details and motivations, to trace big events back to their small human beginnings. No wonder she loved Jane Austen."[1]

Virginia perceived herself as being "outside the magic circle" of Southern Ladyhood. I was surprised by the title of her book. In the foreword Studs Terkel remarks that Virginia's original title for the book was "The Emancipation of Pure White Southern Womanhood." In any case, I was surprised by the vehemence of her rejection of what, to me, she so fully and evidently was. For me, she *was* the magic circle. In her, the "Southern Lady" had come into full expression. In my eyes, it was not that she was emancipated *from* "Southern Womanhood;" rather, she had, in her being, shown what "Southern Womanhood" truly was. She had emancipated *it*.

Virginia and Clifford Durr became very involved with the bus boycott and civil rights activity in Montgomery in the 1950's. Usually it was Virginia who urged her husband to become active: although sympathetic to the cause, he was less inclined to show active solidarity with it.[2] In time, Clifford Durr became one of the few white lawyers in Montgomery willing to represent black clients caught up in the civil rights struggle.

The civil rights movement in Montgomery found in Virginia Durr a woman fully able to understand the implications. She thought that for the South to progress economically and politically it was essential to abolish segregation. The creative receptivity of women like Virginia Durr was an important factor in the budding civil rights movement. It was important for me, too, to see how a woman, confident like Virginia Durr in her role, can make a difference to a cause.

Virginia Durr as a young girl modeled herself on my grandmother. When I was growing up I modeled myself on Virginia Durr. Her liberal ideas, I soon learned, did not alienate her altogether from the ways of the tribe. She always appreciated good manners, principles, traditions, and standards of dress and behavior. Virginia's insistence upon standards clearly distinguished her brand of liberalism from anything that came after in that name. Her encounter, as told in her autobiography, with the skimpily-dressed Joan Baez on one occasion is very telling: "'I think the way you're dressed is absolutely disgraceful. You just told me you're going on a train to Boston, and look at what you've got on. You've got on a bikini and a brassiere and you're barefoot. I think your

---

[1] Jessica Mitford, *Daughters and Rebels*, New York, Avon Books, 1960, p. 231.

[2] "Virginia's friendship with an enlarging circle of black people...and her resultant increasingly frequent confrontations with Southern politicians all served to heighten her radicalism in these years... Much more clearly than did her husband, she believed she was able to see the South for what it was... Her deepening commitment to racial equality, however, had its effect on Cliff's own views on race...etc." John A. Salmond, *The Conscience of a Lawyer: Clifford J. Durr and American Civil Liberties, 1899-1975*, Tuscaloosa, University of Alabama Press, 1990, p. 91-92.

costume is extremely inappropriate. To my mind, it's just not the way to dress to go on a train to Boston.' Oh, she got furious at that."[3]

Virginia was fond of me because she felt we shared a similar experience of Birmingham:

> "I always feel I know you so well because you have had such similar experiences to mine in Birmingham and while you withdrew and I kept at it, and became totally false and dishonest and had some success, still I think it is a damnable system and ruins the human spirit."[4]

It was a theme to which she often returned:

> "I think it is wonderful you have escaped a fate worse than death, that is being a Birmingham debutante or something [of] that order, and I am so delighted and so encouraged that you could see through and reject such a false and horrible set of values."[5]

Still, Virginia's rejection of the falsehoods of Society did not entail rejection of all Southern values. "I am always pleased," she once wrote me, with your loyalty to some of the Southern ways, even if you don't like the system, I agree we have to try and save the best things in the South, while we get rid of the worst things."[6]

Virginia wrote to my father on December 8, 1961, evidently after a visit:

> "I saw what a fine library you had and thought it indicated an inquiring mind. I think the trouble with the South (same old fighting phrase) is the lack of dialogue, while the bases of the society stand like a monolithic rock which cannot be questioned. Exactly the same thing happened in connection with slavery as is happening with segregation, and those of us who do question the sacred institution are renegades and pariahs. Unlike you and Isabel, the powers that be have made up their minds about Cliff and me long ago and we are no longer members of the tribe."

But her last sentence is misleading, for never did she and Cliff ever really feel that they had been expelled from the tribe. That they still "belonged" formed, in her mind, the chief difference between antebellum Montgomery and Reconstruction-era Birmingham. The "money values" that ruled Birmingham were much more cruel, she thought, than those of genteel Montgomery. Birmingham was a much tougher place in which to be on the "other side."

---

[3] Virginia Durr, *Outside the Magic Circle*, edited by Hollinger F. Barnard, University of Alabama, 1985, p. 205.

[4] Letter, Virginia Durr to Caryl Johnston, September 21, 1965.

[5] Letter, Virginia Durr to Caryl Johnston, October 11, 1965.

[6] Letter, Virginia Durr to Caryl Johnston, January 21, 1966.

But Virginia's delight in discovering that Paul Johnston shared her liberal views was beyond doubt real. He was, after all, a member of her tribe. Tribal loyalty was akin to family affection, which, in the South, she wrote, "is one of the best things about us and while they often may make our lives painful at least we don't have the blank vacuum of feeling that I so often sense in people today, who simply have <u>no</u> feelings." Virginia's version of the events in my father's life has its own flavor. This passage is from a letter dated January 21, 1966:

> "I think Paul has been through a hard time, and I get mad at the way these Yankee lawyers tell him he is so wonderful for being so decent and living up to the highest ethics of the Bar, and then not sending him any business, but sending it to some lousy white supremacist lawyer whom they think has pull with City Hall or George Wallace. We went through it and I am not as tolerant and nice as Cliff and Paul, I think it is a rotten [sic] things to do. The Yankees have a very clear division between their pocket books and their principles and never the twain shall meet."

Bob and Jane Coles met the Durrs at a Thanksgiving party at my parents' house in 1962. In a letter of thanks, Coles wrote of Virginia: "She's been through a lot, I gather. Her loneliness comes through. I thought, when talking with her, that she skirts dangerously the edges of bitterness and impracticality... Thank God she is not truly full of despair."

Strange — I think to myself, my perceptions of Virginia were greatly at variance with this description. She never seemed lonely to me, or anywhere near bitter. But then I was young in those days, and susceptible to the charm of her conversation, in which I perceived continuity with the South, rather than discontinuity and ostracism. I was touched to learn, in 1973, that my mother took Virginia to see my grandmother. Evidently the meeting afforded equal pleasure to both. "Nana was very glad to see her," my mother wrote. Whatever those two Southern Ladies found to talk about, their differences of opinion, though considerable on many points, paled beside their fundamental similarity of soul. In the end, they spoke the same language — and it had to do with tribal loyalty and social obligations.

ii. Vulcan

In 1917 a writer from *Collier's* magazine visited Birmingham and noticed the brazen confidence of this steel-making city. He described the prototypical Birmingham businessman of the time as "a big, powerful fellow with an honest blue eye and an expression in which self-confidence, ambition, and power are blended ... and, like Birmingham, he is a little bit naive in the pride of success."[7] These stolid, confident businessmen of early Birmingham built a mon-

---

[7] Quoted in the *Journal of the Birmingham Historical Society*, November, 1982, p. 51.

ument to symbolize Birmingham's role in the Industrial Age when they commissioned in 1903 an Italian sculptor to build the gigantic statue, Vulcan. Vulcan, to the Greeks Hephaestos, was the god of metal-working and forges. In his incarnation as a statue — Birmingham's "Iron Man"— he was placed upon a tower atop Red Mountain, so-called from the color of its iron ore.

Coal, iron, limestone, and water — all the ingredients of steel: these Birmingham possessed in abundance. Virginia Durr once told me she thought Vulcan was a "hard and cruel" symbol. This is true: but "hardness and cruelty" are characteristic of the Industrial Age in many respects. Vulcan was a good symbol of the city for that reason; and Vulcan was to commemorate the steel industry in Birmingham. The city skyline at night was lit for years by the glow of steel furnaces. We could hear the distant hum and clatter of the mills from far away, and the sulphurous smell of smoke lingered long in the air, especially on summer nights.

When I was growing up the powerful lyricism of steel-making was in retreat before another type of process occurring deep in the furnaces of social custom. Black historian Geraldine Moore wrote that "before the sixties [Birmingham] was a city in which two separate and distinct communities existed, and to a large extent, were hostile to each other."[8] It was, others said, "the most segregated city in America."

The segregation ordinances that divided white and black had mostly been passed during the 1920's, at which time, according to William Nunnelley, the Ku Klux Klan boasted some 20,000 members. After the Second World War, as blacks began to press forward with the call for equal rights, bombs began exploding in Birmingham. From 1955 to 1965, there were some fifty-four bombings or attempt bombings, the worst of which was at the Sixteenth Street Baptist church on September 15, 1963, in which four Negro girls were killed, and scores injured.

For a time, everyone was blaming everyone else for what had happened. A lot of people blamed the "outside agitators," those college students who were coming down in droves to create social justice. Some of the segregationists blamed the Negroes, saying they did it to make the whites look bad. The black community was bitter and outraged, feeling that the unsolved bombings indicated the collusion of the police with the Klan. Robert Chambliss, the Klansman indicted for his role in the 16th St. Church bombing, blamed Gary Thomas Rowe. From his seclusion in Kilby Prison, he said that "Rowe was the head leader in all the bombings in and around Birmingham... because every time that anything [happened] he would come back to the meetings and brag about it, brag about he done such and such."[9]

---

[8] William A. Nunnelley, *Bull Connor,* University of Alabama, 1991, p. 5.

[9] Chambliss' accusations were later corroborated when scandals broke out concerning Rowe in the 1980's. Apparently the FBI did know of violence against blacks committed by its paid informers. A *New York Times* report "detailed several incidents of violence involving Rowe which allegedly were known to his FBI superiors. But 'as long as he was providing good intelligence, the

Rowe, on the other hand, blamed the Police Department and the FBI. The Alabama Department of Public Safety came out with a long report about Communist influence in the Freedom Rider movement. A Mr. Fisher, of White Citizen's Council persuasion, blamed the City Councillors — "They are like drunk men who are on one side of the road one day and on the other side the next... Maybe the yellow line is down their backs."[10]

And so it went. The finger-pointing turned in whatever direction lay opposite from the pointer's unassailable "true North." But the speech, and later the book, that blamed everybody was Charles Morgan's *A Time to Speak* (1964). Morgan blamed everyone from the political leadership down through the professional ranks of ministers, lawyers, journalists, businessmen and even ordinary citizens. "Birmingham is not a dying city," he pronounced, "It is dead."

The nonviolent ideal of the early black civil-rights movement was put to a severe test in Birmingham. But by 1963, when the demonstrations occurred in Birmingham, some new elements had entered into the struggle. David J. Garrow writes that the year 1961 marked the change from a mass movement to one that actively sought the involvement and protection of the Federal government.[11] Secondly, after the failure of King's nonviolent campaign in Albany, Georgia, the campaign in Birmingham was planned with the idea of provoking — albeit nonviolently — a confrontation.

Birmingham's Police Commissioner, Bull Connor, was the ideal target. Birmingham at the time was in the throes of electing a new city government. Connor was replaced by the more moderate Albert Boutwell. Yet Connor insisted on being allowed to serve out his term of office — basing his claim on a 1959 city act that said that incumbents should be allowed to serve their full term. Martin Luther King planned his Project C — the Birmingham confrontation — around these events. Some people criticized the marchers for not waiting until Boutwell had a chance to prove himself. At the time the marches finally began, Birmingham had two leaders — Connor, still in office, and Boutwell, who had not yet in a real sense arrived. "Goading the bull" became an irresistible part of the marchers' plan.

The stage was set for confusion. Everyone now knows the result: Bull Connor's police force spraying hoses and letting loose attack dogs on peaceful demonstrators. Flashed to all points around the world on May 4, 1963, this

---

Birmingham field office was willing to overlook Rowe's own involvement,' the *Times* quoted the report as saying." The family of Mrs. Viola Greg Liuzzo later brought suit against Rowe, claiming that he had played a part in the slaying of Mrs. Liuzzo. *The Berkshire Eagle*, February 18, 1980. Indeed, the whole Rowe business belonged to a past about which my father did not want to speak. The revelations of Rowe's participation in Klan violence deeply disturbed him.

[10] Material in this paragraph quoted from my general introduction to the "Birmingham, Ala. Police Department Surveillance Files, 1947-1980," which I compiled as a library intern for the Birmingham Public Library; Accession 1125.

[11] David J. Garrow, *Bearing the Cross: Martin Luther King, Jr. and the Southern Christian Leadership Conference*, New York, 1988, p. 157.

sight became the symbol of symbols of the civil rights struggle. Charles Evers, the brother of slain civil rights worker Medgar Evers, decried what had happened in Birmingham. "A disaster," he called it. [12] But he was referring to the violence and bloodshed in Birmingham, not to the symbolism.

I too think that what happened in Birmingham was a disaster — but also from the point of view of symbolism. After Birmingham, no longer could the struggle for civil rights be seen as a common struggle of white *and* black. From Birmingham on, inevitably, it was white *against* black. What happened in Birmingham was to prove a major stumbling-block to the effort to forge a common remembrance. The sight of policemen spraying peaceful demonstrators is a reactive and media-driven event rather than being a self-confident and self-created symbol. In thinking there is an interplay between whole and part, between relating (integration) and identifying (separation). We distinguish in order to relate; we relate in order to distinguish. This dynamic interplay, this call-and-response between whole and part, gives thinking its movement, its 'ecology.' But "Birmingham" — i.e., Bull Connor and his dogs — arrested this thinking process in mid-air. A big problem, for the black community after Birmingham, was that of being suspended between "Integration" and "Separation" and not being able to choose between them.

This was not the case with the movement's bold beginning. At the commencement of the Montgomery bus boycott, Martin Luther King gave a remarkable speech, in which he sounded the first strains of a powerful new symbolism. On December 5, 1955, he said: "If we protest courageously, and yet with dignity and Christian love, when the history books are written in the future, somebody will have to say, 'There lived a race of people, of black people, who had the moral courage to stand up for their rights. And thereby they injected new meaning into the veins of history and civilization.'" [13]

The "veins of history"! History as a Living Being! This is extraordinary — but not just because it concerns people fighting for their rights. That is not new. What is new is that those who were fighting were *black*. This was the "new meaning" that was to be injected into the veins of history. Nothing less than an entire readjustment of the view of history would be necessary to accommodate the coming-into-being of black identity. This is symbol-making on a grand scale — and it comes from a forge every bit as deep as Vulcan's. But because it was so deep few could understand it. Ironically, Bull Connor was one of the few who did. In an unsuccessful 1962 bid for the governorship, Connor said: "Our people in the South want to see him [i.e. the Negro] rise and we want to see him go just as high as he can and as fast as he can. He must realize, however, that no man can instill manhood and character into another. He must do that for himself."[14]

---

[12] Robert Penn Warren, *Who Speaks for the Negro?* New York, Random House, 1965, p. 229.

[13] Stephen B. Oates, *Let the Trumpet Sound: The Life of Martin Luther King, Jr.* New York, Harper & Row, 1982, p. 71.

[14] Nunnelley, *Bull Connor*, University of Alabama, p. 123.

Martin Luther King also knew that the civil-rights movement was more than a struggle for rights. There was more to it than that. Why? Because the black struggle was different from that of other people. The deeper issue for the blacks was the problem of identity — of origins — of spiritual paternity. [15] Still, the tool lying closest to hand in the struggle was the promise of the Declaration of Independence — that "all men are created equal." At the time this phrase was penned, it meant that Americans should have the same rights as Englishmen. "The word *equality* does not appear in the Constitution of the United States — except for a reference to equality among the states," remarks Eugene Genovese in *The Southern Front* (1995). Also, he reminds us, "the egalitarian ideology of the French Revolution cannot legitimately be read into the founding of the American Republic." Nevertheless, equality has come to mean, in the United States, equality between persons. But when the leaders of the civil rights struggle took up the issue of equality, they did something new with it. They brought something to it from their unique spiritual history. One may say that they *Christianized* it: they took a leap — supernaturally; they originated themselves symbolically; in their hands equality became the teaching of revelatory brotherhood. [16]

It was a tremendous achievement: a social and political re-enactment of that moment in the life of Christ when he said –

I and the Father are one! (John 10:30)

This confession of union is the great secret of our civilization — perhaps of any civilization. It is what allows things to go on — that the children can incorporate the memories of the fathers, that things learned can be passed on, that there can be a heritage. It was the covenantal idea brought forth in new historical circumstances.

But the events of Birmingham clouded the tremendous question of black identity. Very little notice, in fact, was taken of the spiritual deed of the blacks, other than perfunctory notices that the "Black churches had a lot to do with it." As Richard John Neuhaus remarks, the media was keen on confrontation. Neuhaus once met with Dr. King, who told him: "They [i.e. the media] aren't interested in the *why* of what we're doing, only the *what*...and because they don't understand the why they cannot really understand the what."[17] And even

---

[15] Robert Penn Warren asked Wyatt Tee Walker, Executive Director of the SCLC, if the Negro's discovery of identity was a part of the whole movement. Walker agreed that it was "a very critical part." Warren, *op.cit.,* p. 222.

[16] The ideal of Christian brotherhood was well stated by Fred Shuttlesworth, head of the Alabama Christian Movement for Civil Rights — "We only pray that *our* methods will always be Christian, that no hate will ever be found or practiced in our hearts and actions, and that out of the intensity of the struggle we Negroes will become more religious, more consecrated, better Americans." From "The Alabama Christian Movement for Human Rights and the Birmingham Struggle for Civil Rights, 1956-1963," by Glenn T. Eskew, in *Birmingham, Alabama, 1956-1963: in The Black Struggle for Civil Rights,* edited by David J. Garrow, Brooklyn, N.Y., 1989.

[17] Richard John Neuhaus, *The Naked Public Square*, Eerdman's Publishers, 1984, p. 98.

as late as 1990, a historian could virtually efface the Christian basis of this movement by writing that "the Rev. Martin Luther King, Jr., went on to become the most important black leader of this century, the very embodiment of the notion that change can come in a nonrevolutionary way, using the political process, reinforced by mobilizing the people in peaceful demonstrations of protest." [18]

It was not only the white liberal, of course, who helped to efface Christianity from the civil-rights movement. [19] Robert Coles recalled meeting a young man disturbed by the "sudden, sad break-up of the 'old' civil rights movement, five years after it was born, with much attendant acrimony. My friend was especially hurt by all the suspiciousness and rancor which, out of nowhere, it seemed, spread into the discourse of men and women supposedly brothers and sisters in a common social and political effort."[20] Robert Coles' young man may be referring to the Black Power movement. What was the need that Stokeley Carmichael — the leader of the Black Power movement — and others felt they had to address? It was the very issue that had been driven out by the passion of Birmingham, the issue of *black identity*. But it soon took the form of the issue of *power*. Stokeley Carmichael believed that "Power is the only thing respected in the world and we must get it at any cost." Looking King in the eye, he continued: "Martin, you know as well as I do that practically every other ethnic group in America has done just this [i.e. gain power]. The Jews, the Irish and the Italians did it, why can't we?"

King replied: "That is just the point. No one has ever heard the Jews publicly chant a slogan of Jewish power, but they have power. Through group identity, determination and creative endeavor, they have gained it... This is exactly what we must do... But this must come through a program, not a slogan."[21]

Other immigrant groups, having a cohesive cultural identity, fitted more readily in the ongoing march of Western history. But history — as we have seen — was the point at issue for the blacks. They could not so readily join the ongoing march at the end of the line, as other immigrant groups had done. For

---

[18] John A. Salmond, *The Conscience of a Lawyer, Clifford J. Durr and American Civil Liberties, 1899-1975;* University of Alabama Press, 1990, p. 175.

[19] Commentary on the civil-rights era sometimes seems to divide along lines of a Christian realism versus utopian expectationism. For example, in *Carry Me Home*, Diane McWhorter faults the local newspapers for failing to report local news in the 1960's. True. If you wanted to find out what was going on back then, you read *The New York Times,* not the *Birmingham News.* Why? Because the community really was going through drastic changes. People, like animals when wounded, have the impulse to crawl into the bushes. The silence of local newspapers attests to the genuineness of the change being experienced. A Christian realism does not demand self-transformation *at the same time* as self-examination — for that is like asking life and death to coexist simultaneously. It's not unreasonable, of course, to expect great things from people. It's only unreasonable when the things expected are contrary to one another.

[20] Robert Coles, *Yale Review,* Winter, 1984, p. 312-13.

[21] Stephen Oates, *Let the Trumpet Sound,* 1982, p. 401.

them natural, cultural, racial history was not enough. In this history there was the remembrance of slavery. The bitterness of this remembrance hindered the search for black identity and blocked it at the door of the past.

A stark situation indeed, and one not demanded of other people who had had to fight for their rights. Black Power became for some a way of working out of this cultural impasse — of finding a 'natural history.' But the point of the civil rights movement that culminated with Birmingham was, it seems to me, that it showed the uselessness of merely 'natural' history. The real power of that movement was its discovery of what could be called *resurrectional* history — a history sprung from the very death of the past.

Here is a fitting extension of the symbolism of Vulcan's torch! In the crucible of Birmingham the old and the new history came to grips with each other. The old history of economics and manufacture yielded to the new realization that history is the *industry of mankind*.

But it was to be a concept for a far-distant future. Birmingham, an apparent victory for civil rights, was an actual defeat for this new history as the industry of mankind. "I and the Father are one!" This is the gateway into historical consciousness. It is the concept of the *patrimony* – ridiculed and maligned by that other movement that also claimed rights and liberation and found that the easiest means of doing so was to jump on the back of the black civil rights movement. [22]

The feminists effectively slammed shut that patrimonial gate for anyone audacious enough to go looking for it. But this was not the only betrayal of the civil rights movement, not the only instance in which its spiritual energies were deflected into *power* rather than *patrimony*.

Condemnation is an adolescent gesture people sometimes make when they first discover the past. Most of us go through it in one form or another on our way towards greater integration and historical consciousness. But in modern politics the idolization of self-interest has combined with ethnic, racial, national or gender awareness to construct a near-permanent state of condemnation. The arrested maturity characteristic of this state is symptomatic of how the patrimonial energies can become malignant and destructive when subordinated to political agendas. History as a *Living Being* has yet to find its compelling symbol, its point of entry into a specifically *American* history. We are faced, more than thirty years later, with the necessity for coming to grips with the real dimensions of the unfinished symbolical struggle: the struggle to reclaim the patrimony, the spiritual basis of Western history.

White liberals almost universally agreed that for the South to progress economically it was necessary to abolish the offensive segregation system. But Martin Luther King, Fred Shuttlesworth, and even the editor of the black newspaper, *The Birmingham World* — Emory O. Jackson, who in some ways

---

[22] See: F. Carolyn Graglia, *Domestic Tranquillity*, Spence Publishing, Dallas, Texas. She says that the feminist movement "piggybacked" on the civil rights movement by claiming victim status for women.

opposed the unfolding civil rights movement — took the movement to a higher stage. They were concerned with big questions like history and spirit. As a result, they began to pay attention to the character of Western civilization as a whole. What was it to be a person of color in white, Western civilization? What is the moral worth of that civilization, given its history with respect to those same persons of color? Questions like these have an all-too-familiar ring now. But why? Who gets the credit? Not Martin Luther King and his contemporaries — who not only asked the questions but provided a spiritually-affirming answer to them.

Thanks to the biggest act of theft and intellectual deceit that has ever been perpetrated in recent years, the fruit of wisdom was stolen from those who had labored for it. I refer to the famous, or infamous, deconstruction movement, in which European intellectuals and their American counterparts in the 1970's started raising questions about the moral worth of Western civilization. The deconstructionists, as they called themselves, essentially stole the spiritual fruit of the civil rights struggle, which was the rediscovery of Western spirituality. Where the black men had pondered these questions and gave the answer of nonviolence and forbearance in the moment of crisis, the intellectual elite could not disguise their glee at having gotten hold of a potent acid for corroding the fabric of society. [23]

Glenn Loury calls the political correctness and West-bashing that resulted from the deconstructive critique a form of "seductive intellectual nihilism." And although he discusses the political correctness, intellectual timidity, and conformity that characterize American intellectual life, he does not make a link, so far as I am aware, with the civil rights movement. Yet it seems to me that link can be made. For behind the quest for political participation, the big questions hovered. To have followed through with the answers given by Jackson, King, and Shuttlesworth and many black civic and religious leaders, could have led to a deepened affirmation of who we are — on the part of both black and white America. But this is not what happened. Instead the whole debate soured. It became a tirade of race and power. What could have been a challenge and a spur to American thinking instead became a fraudulent exercise of "tenured radicals."

There is a fitting epitaph to this betrayal of the real meaning of the civil rights movement — and one pronounced by Rev. Fred Shuttlesworth himself. The occasion was a Nov. 2, 1998, symposium at the Sixteenth Street Baptist Church in Birmingham, held to commemorate the recent publication of the Birmingham Historical Society's book, *A Walk to Freedom: the Rev. Fred Shuttlesworth and the Alabama Christian Movement for Human Rights*. Rev.

---

[23] One must admit that W.E.B. DuBois provided a bridge to the deconstructionist attack. Glenn Loury remarks in his *One by One from the Inside Out* (1995) that "...one cannot avoid the fact that by the end of his life, DuBois was a bitter antagonist of American interests in the international arena, an unabashed apologist for global Communism, and an ardent exponent of that anti-Western animus so prominent a part of the ideology of today's 'progressives.'"

Shuttlesworth heard the speeches by historians illustrating the various aspects of the dynamic movement that he led with Rev. King. Afterwards he got up to say a few words himself.

Perhaps it was a kind of benediction, or warning. He said: "What writers see and don't see, God sees."

Nana ("Miss Clara"), 1965

IX. Promise of Generations

There have been two attempts to write the life of General John Hartwell Cocke. The first was begun over seventy years ago. The typescript lies in one of those gray dust-free manuscript boxes which, with its hundreds of fellows, now crowd the shelves of archival libraries and do service for the preservation of our culture. Students and scholars find their way to such collections when they intend to exhume a piece of the past, — like deep-sea divers submerging themselves beneath the surface of the rows and rows of gray waves. The elegance of this piece of writing is in contrast to its rough typewritten form — unpaged, portions crossed out — which today already looks old-fashioned. It was written before the era of word-processing; the struggles of the writer are much more evident on the page. The man who wrote this biography did not live to finish it.

The second attempt to write a biography of the Old General came to pass in my lifetime. How far that project advanced, where those pages lie, I do not know. That history too was broken off before it was completed, though this time the cause was not death, but love. A man — I will call him James Elmhurst — began this task, thinking that the past was safely behind him, that all it involved was research, scholarship, and writing — for which his years of training and study had well prepared him.

He had no idea, as he drove to Bremo on that July day in 1968, that history was about to play a joke on him. He was about to be hoisted — out of scholarship, footnotes, acknowledgements, manuscript boxes. He was to be hoisted out of history and thrown into the Story. History, in fact, had not stopped happening. It was not behind him, and safe. It was present now, and dangerous.

Indeed, a man in his time of life can be in a dangerous phase. He was at the second of his moon-nodes, his 38th year, a time of "sacrifice, expulsion, or death." It is not that "sacrifice, expulsion or death" do not happen at other times, at any time, of our lives. But those that happen in conjunction with the eighteen-year rhythm can carry a particular quality of revelation.   James Elmhurst's mission on that particular day was simply to pay another visit to General Cocke's great-granddaughter, Mrs. Forney Johnston. Mrs. Johnston made yearly summer visits to Bremo and was only too happy to play the part of hostess, muse and mentor to Mr. Elmhurst's scholarly labors, which she was eager to encourage. She fretted much, in fact, during her declining years about this biography of General Cocke, which she was most anxious to see before she quitted the shining lands of mortality.

It was not to be. Her granddaughter was visiting at the time, a young lady on whom I bestow the fictionalized name of "Miss M." Indeed, I protectively clothe "Miss M." with the sound of that consonant that opens moon, mute, mystery. She was eighteen years younger than James Elmhurst: at that phase of the soul's becoming where, as one spiritual biographer tells us, there can be a "window into future destiny." Whatever Mr. Elmhurst's own romantic history may have been — or whether the love of his task was suspended, at that crucial moment, by the appearance of another object — he — they— became enamoured. Perhaps the living room at Bremo, where they first met, had something to do with it. It is a 22-foot cube, a fortress of containment, where glances and whispers wear an aura of echoes. Historians tell us what happens; poets, on the other hand, speak of the romance of destiny. But history is also part of destiny, and often in what happens there is more than a little romance.

That Bremo should have been the setting for this particular twist on history — that old General Cocke's great-great-great-granddaughter should have been blocking the path of this latest and most hopeful biographer — it fits the requirements of Story, but it leaves history-writing in the shade. Catastrophic — as far as the biography of General Cocke is concerned — a shipwreck of scholarship.

History fled into the shadows while Mr. Elmhurst and Miss M. sorted out their problems of free will and resolved whatever existed between them, for good or ill. In the weeks and months and years that followed this meeting, there were letters, declarations, proposal, acceptance. *"I pressed for a commitment to marriage because I felt it was, paradoxically, the only way I could court you,"* James Elmhurst wrote to Miss M., explaining it to himself, to her, long after it was all over. James Elmhurst was a devotee of the romantic mysticism of Charles Williams, which Miss M., being young, could hardly appreciate. The tolling bells of Exchange and Substitution, the Vision of Beatrice, Co-inherence, the flash and the prolongation — what kind of sense could this make to a girl just barely a college freshman? *"Your need for me is killing me,"* she wrote him once, cruel in her youth, her freedom, her lack of need.

Two years later, she broke it off — in an eruption as sudden as it was final. She who had agreed to marry now disagreed and ended it. Poor Mr. Elmhurst! He tried to piece together the shattered fragments of reason and love: *"As to what had happened to you I could only guess: the closest you came to explanation was simply that love had lessened (although I guessed some spiritual experience was working at a deeper level); and we both waited and watched to see how the wind might list."* An odd expression, that —*"we both waited and watched to see how the wind might list."* What else was there to do but "wait and watch" for the final dismissal? There is some nobility of character in those words, I think — some glimmer of *amor fati*.

The love affair and its unhappy ending caused, for James, a fatal interruption of his project. He never took it up again once the affair had ended. The unwritten biography became for him the story of lost love. Perhaps it pained him too much to remember. General Cocke sank once again beneath the swell of gray boxes.

* * *

It was not, as I have said, the first attempt. Armistead Gordon began a biography of Cocke some sixty years ago, but died before it was completed. While mowing his grass on a hot day in Charlottesville, he suffered a fatal heart attack. The first biographer dead, the second cast out through love: the story of the Cocke biography makes an ill-starred history.

No published book has been written on the life of General Cocke.[1] His life, in merciful dispensation, has been spared the second death — that of modern academic "treatment." I think he would have wanted it that way: either say nothing, or tell the story in its spiritual dimensions. Stand by the Cross, or stand not at all.

The cock, according to Madge Childs, is a symbol of Christ: "The lordly ruler of the grounded flock, the cock with his crowned head, his iridescent feathers... is a Christian symbol, found specifically in the story of Jesus Christ's trial before Pontius Pilate... [It is] the egoic earth bird that announces the sunlight of a new day, as the Golgotha Event in evolution proclaimed the dawn of the resurrecting power."[2] That the herald of the dawn — the cock — is also a gutter term for the male organ is more than an accident of language. Here is the opportunity to confront the charge, made by deconstructionists, feminists, modernists and assorted intellectual malcontents, that Western history is nothing but "phallocentrism." It is very odd that such a group of nominalists, who believe that words are arbitrary and do not refer to anything real, yet exalt the "phallus" to be the prime perpetrator of everything they hate. Suddenly they abandon their nominalism and become diehard realists — i.e., believing that words *do refer* to real things. But the hatred of the "patrimony" is not merely an accusation of male dominance — which, to these people, undercuts any claim regarding the moral worth of Western history. It is fundamentally an

---

[1] Also noted by Stuart L. Butler, in his "General Cocke in the War of 1812," from the *Magazine of Albemarle County History* (2007) – in his Endnotes he comments, "Surprisingly, there is no comprehensive published biography of John Hartwell Cocke."

[2] Madge Childs, *Hamlet: Through the Valley of the Shadow*, Atlanta, Ga., Curtiss Printing co., 1980, p. 115.

attack against humanistic biography — the idea of individuality. [3] For the rejection of the patrimony brings with it the rejection of the way patrimony has been grounded in history, that is, the *matrimony*, which can be called "God's Compact with Woman." Matrimony – the Legitimacy Principle[4] — incorporates the symbolic dimension, in the sense that a human birth becomes not just a biological incident, but an event with biographical significance. For: *which family? which birth?* This question would be of great significance to a soul seeking to be born! The matrimonial compact thus points to the fabric of human destiny. Matrimony is the institution which, more than any other, attests to the fact that physical, material and biological factors alone are not sufficient to plumb the depths of human existence.

Let the crowing of the cock herald the new dawn of understanding of this natural-supernatural fact.

* * *

After the ending of the love affair, James had written to Miss M.: "*[I guessed] some spiritual experience was working at a deeper level...*"

Indeed it was. The reader may have guessed by now the identity of Miss M., whose guilt at being the unwitting instrument of the shipwreck of the Cocke biography I will not dwell upon. Suffice it to say that it took many years before the waters of memory retreated enough to reveal a bare patch of land. The task of cultivating this little plot of history fell to me.

Rather: the way was left open for me to choose this task. About thirty years elapsed between James Elmhurst's relinquishment of his task and my taking up the task of writing this book. Here is the "generational number" — for there are roughly thirty years' difference between one generation and the next. This generational number is the critical term most often omitted in discussions about freedom and determinism. Freedom means little more than self-will if there is no historical background to take into account. There must be *something* to limit, something to look back on or measure up against. On the other hand, if there is *only* the script, — only the "march of history" —

---

[3] Cf. On the deconstructionist Paul de Man: he "...shared with the structuralists the determination to make the psychological understanding of action ashamed of itself. There must be no talk of self, identity, mind, imagination, or will: these are sentimentalities, tokens of an axiomatic humanism." Denis Donoghue, "The Limits of Language," in *The New Republic,* July 7, 1986.

[4] The Legitimacy Principle – "every child must have a father." Hence: "In the civilized society the females accept the regulation of their sexuality on the basis of the Sexual Constitution – monogamous marriage, the Legitimacy Principle, the double standard and female loyalty and chastity; in the primitive society the female reject sexual regulation and embrace the Promiscuity Principle, a woman's right to control her own sexuality." Daniel Amneus, *The Garbage Generation: The Consequences of the Destruction of the Two-Parent Family and the Need to Stabilize It by Strengthening Its Weakest Link, the Father's Role.* Alhambra, CA 1990. I agree with Amneus's analysis but take the question of legitimacy a step further. It is the spiritual reality that is decisive; the Legitimacy Principle points to the difference between reproduction, common to all of life, and procreation, unique to mankind.

one's individual contribution cannot amount to much. It is a mere repetition of the masque of the ancestors — or of whatever determinant occupies the stage at the moment: race, class, gender, genes, nationality, religion, folk souls, ideologies, ideas, material processes or spiritual beings.

What is this 'pause' — this interval — in human life which makes it possible to speak both of script and initiative? This is the *blooded colt* — about which I will have something to say at the end of this chapter.

But before I speak of it, I must join a few more threads of this narrative. One of those threads has to do with my grandmother Clara, who carried her disappointment at the unfulfillment of the Cocke biography to the grave. How much she knew of my particular role in the shipwreck of her hopes I will never know. She never spoke of it to me. The family disappointment, such as I understood it, sank beneath the waves, leaving little eddies and hints of disapproval.

But there were other times when my grandmother did share her memories and hopes with me. And one of those times allows me the opportunity to tell another little story-within-a-story having to do with the generational covenant. One summer afternoon at Bremo, my grandmother suggested that I take down some of her recollections. We sat on the front porch and she gazed with her failing eyesight out towards the lawn; I sat with a notebook on my knee. She spoke collectedly and in full sentences, and not too fast. What I wrote down (unfortunately we did not get too far with it) I later typed up; it made a ten-page typescript.

"My very first memory is of a tall man standing by an open fire, perhaps the dining room at Lower Bremo, where a large wood fire was often kept burning. I was lifted by my father in his arms and called his darling little daughter." Her father died when she was four years old. Clara's mother had much to manage with the raising of seven children alone, and in the course of a few years Col. Pollard, her mother's father, suggested that the family go to live in Sewanee, Tennessee. Col. Pollard was one of the founders of the University of the South, and he thought that the children would benefit from the educational opportunities of living there.

In the spring of 1887 Clara, then about seven, moved to Sewanee with her family. Eighty years later Clara recalled their house there, within walking distance of the College, their Scots governess, the walks in the woods and the donkey rides. The children attended services at the University Chapel:

> "One of the lasting impressions were those made by our attendance at the University Chapel... The chaplain was Mr. Gailor, who afterwards became presiding bishop of the Episcopal Church and a very noted preacher. When he became bishop, he said he was called upon to preach in many of the great cathedrals in England, and on great occasions in this country and elsewhere. There was one famous sermon he preached to the graduating class, and he said he was asked to preach this sermon many times. I still remember the sermon and can repeat part of it. The text of the sermon

was from a poem, 'The mill will never grind with water that is past.' The opportunities that arise in life are never repeated; every day should be one of constructive effort. One should always aspire to higher character and achievement."

In recording this part of my grandmother's recollections, I was struck, not only by what she remembered so clearly after eighty-some years, but with the many-layered irony of it. That the most popular sermon of a Christian preacher should take up the theme of the very unchristian idea of Eternal Return, the Wheel of Becoming, was not the least of it. But more to the point, my grandmother's generation, which came to adulthood around 1900, lived at the high crest of the belief in Progress. [5] As in the image of the water mill, belief in Progress often implied a rejection of the past. But for my grandmother to have taken it so would be manifestly impossible. That she could not see the contradiction both touched and alarmed me. For she was, to all of us children, the very incarnation of Tradition: matriarch, mistress of Bremo, Colonial Dame, Southern Gentlewoman. My brother Paul describes her influence upon him in his "Spiritual Autobiography":

"At the center of life at Bremo, exerting a moral force that like gravity had the capacity to curve space, was my grandmother, Clara, known to all grandchildren, and to all servants when they were out of her earshot, as Nana. Nana had a strong influence on me — but her influence was not like that of the men of my family. The men influenced me indirectly, by what they were and did, whereas Nana, working directly, read poetry to me when I was young, and seemed to care about my moral education... She believed in the efficacy of a good talking-to, and the phrases she used and re-used will always affect me in complex ways. She would say to me: 'There are standards for us the same as the Greeks,' and also, 'You are of a family that serves by leading' as well as 'Duty is the most sublime word in the English language' — the last, incidentally, a direct quote from Robert E. Lee. On the surface, and under the influence of my father, who dismissed Nana as a product of the Nineteenth Century, I discounted her, but in fact she got through in ways I am only just beginning now to figure out."

---

[5] "For...we have been moving on by the momentum of nineteenth-century ideas of 'progress'...which is why 'progressive' is *the* most unexceptionable adjective and 'reactionary' *the* most universally condemned one..." John Lukacs, *Historical Consciousness*, 1985, p. 41. Cf. also the 1947 entry in the Journals of Ludwig Wittgenstein: "The truly apocalyptic view of the world is that things do *not* repeat themselves. It isn't absurd e.g. to believe that the age of science and technology is the beginning of the end for humanity; that the idea of great progress is a delusion, along with the idea that the truth will ultimately be known; that there is nothing good or desirable about scientific knowledge and that mankind in seeking it, is falling into a trap. It is by no means obvious that this is not how things are." From *Culture and Value,* edited by H. Von Wright, Chicago, 1980.

My brother and I felt very strongly the break between the generations. This break was not so much between us and our parents — that came later — as between our parents and their parents. The geological divide lay one generation back, and this created a confusion in our minds. Paul's "Spiritual Autobiography" continues:

> "When I graduated from college and set forth on the path of life, I was confused. From my father I had received a liberalism that was open, questioning, abrupt, intellectually energetic but associated in my mind with alcoholic excess and family chaos; from my grandparents I received a conservatism that was inward- and backward-looking, but linked in my mind with settings of grace and beauty."

Our father had revolted: were we to revolt from the revolter, and if so, what would be the result? Would the road lead back to the affirmations of our grandparents, or would it be a long march to nowhere, an endless playing at revolt?

I had another curious connection with Sewanee, Tennessee, in 1987, when I was living in Birmingham. It had to do with learning about another one of these revolters from a revolter, only in this case the revolt lasted for two generations. My husband, while browsing in the Birmingham Public Library one day, came across a curious book, which had not been checked out for some forty-five years. Entitled *The Angelic Mysteries of the Nine Heavens,* its author was Kenneth Sylvan [Launfals] Guthrie [1871-1941], who was identified as a teacher in the Extension School at the University of the South, in Sewanee, Tennessee.

My interest piqued, I wrote to Sewanee University to inquire into particulars concerning Kenneth Guthrie. I found out that he had graduated from the University at about the time my grandmother had been living there as a child, that is, about 1890, and that he was considered remarkable by persons who knew him. He was born in Dundee, Scotland, and had several degrees from other American universities. He was the author of several books, including *The Communion with God* (1895), *The Philosophy of Plotinus* (1896) and *The Spiritual Message of Literature* (1909).

The full title of the book that Robert brought back for us to look was this: *The Angelic Mysteries of the Nine Heavens, A Drama of Interior Initiation, Embodying Dionysius the Areopagite's Ninefold Celestial Hierarchy, A Vision of Judgment and Heaven, An Evocation of the Historic Lawgivers, The Reincarnating Career of a Famous Soul, A Passage through Hell, Purgatory & Heaven and the Mystery of the Twenty-four Elders.* This work was published circa 1925 by the Platonist Press of Yonkers, New York. It contains an arresting passage about Christianity:

> "As anointed means '<u>endued with breath</u>,'
> <u>Christ</u> Jesus means Jesus '<u>caused to breathe</u>,'

A title only given unto him
After he learned to breathe interiorly.
Therefore the <u>Christians</u> really <u>breathers</u> means,
And Christian Church thus means the <u>Breathing Church.</u>"

This etymology of the word 'anointed' may not be correct. And even if it were correct, this description of Christianity seems to have more of promise than of actuality. But there is something to think about here. My question is: how do people 'breathe' in history, and is there a relationship between Christianity and this 'breathing'? How do human beings achieve historical consciousness? In my discussion of Martin Luther King in the previous chapter, I pointed to his famous speech in 1955 where he talked about "new meaning in the veins of history" — he pointed to history as a Living Being. I believe King spoke a truth — or, to put in a different language — he created a symbol of great spiritual power. In the accession of spiritual power blacks achieved a new surge of historical consciousness. 'Spiritual power' is the inward or inner counterpart of historical consciousness. It is a kind of deep or interior breathing carried on by means of thinking, symbolism, action.

Regarding Kenneth Sylvan Guthrie, I should not fail to mention the kind response to my inquiries from Elizabeth Chitty, Associate Historiographer of the University of the South. She wrote to me on July 9, 1987, saying that "Kenneth Guthrie was the grandson of a famous lady Fanny Wright who established a pre-Civil War utopian experiment named Nashoba, near Memphis, which failed..."

Here indeed is material for a generational story! I could understand why Kenneth Guthrie went in quest for the hierarchical spiritual company, for I myself was embarked on a similar quest. Fanny Wright, Guthrie's grandmother, was a leveler. In perceiving the inequalities of class and race she failed to see the tyranny in wanting to make the world over in her own image. Kenneth Guthrie's mother was the first defector. It was a revolt lasting two generations: for both of her Sylvia Guthrie's sons became ministers — a choice of vocation which, according to O.B. Emerson, Sylvia Guthrie was proud of. It was a commitment "very, very far from the free ideals that made for her mother a world of her own."

* * *

Midge Decter, in her *Liberal Parents, Radical Children*, remarks on the downward mobility of children such as we were. She called us "a generation that refused to be tested."

Much has been written about the generation that came to maturity in the 1960's. Depending upon the perspective, these accounts are either laudatory or hostile. As far as I was concerned, the Sixties were about the spiritual search, which came about as the result of the experience of discontinuity. The first experience of discontinuity, for my brother and me, was that which existed between our parents and our grandparents. We were a part of both of these worlds, but belonged to neither. We both sought for a return to history, for continuity in history. But by the time we tried to return to the fold, the fold had folded. How could we find a sense of history, or of tradition, or of legitimate authority, in the programs of Big Government and Big Business — whose collusion was littering the American landscape with a scum of highways, gas stations, and fast food joints? The country had been hollowed out. All that was left was politics and commerce.

It was a second casting-out. First was exile from family, later the exile from country. For me, the realization that the fold had folded sparked a spiritual journey. I realized that what I sought lay hidden in history's deeper channels, its underground caverns and springs of thought.

I graduated from college in 1970. Between graduation from college and marriage I had fourteen years. Fourteen years to "refuse to be tested."

What is my gift to the world from those fourteen years? If I had any singular idea at all, it would be this: to act, to find one's task, involves first learning how to think. And this takes a long time, a long period of emulation, training, experience, and reflection. Many have pointed to "instant gratification" as the bane of our youth, of our economy, of our culture. They point to the shortened attention span of young people, to the absence of moral stamina among their elders, to the inability of society to affirm endurance as a moral value. But the refusal of premature fulfillment has become, to my mind, more than a moral value. It forms the metaphysical keystone of human life.

For what, indeed, is the meaning of *concentration*, of *gathering-in*, of *training* this vehicle of horse-flesh, of *liberally educating* this horse-intelligence, unless, in a sense, the best is for the last, unless *waiting* makes sense — unless *ripening* has a meaning in human life? This is why man is a 'Blooded Colt' among the earth's creatures — why even natural man, with respect to earth's creatures, is a thoroughbred. The baby in the womb is *waiting*; the child in elementary school is *waiting*; the horse tossing his mane in the paddock, proud and high-stepping, is *waiting!* And all of these are gathering their forces according to the needs of the time in which they find themselves — learning their steps, gaining purposes and skills according to their talents, their heritage, their blood. There can be no sense of purpose in a purely natural world. Refinement and discipline are supernatural qualities for the thoroughbred in man.

Time is parceled out, with man, as *timing*. Thinking develops, not evenly, not uniformly, but in spurts, halts, hurdles and braces, according to the *pace of life*. The most anyone can say of himself, herself — "I am in training!" Training? For what? *I am in training to live my life!*

The regenerate man keeps his thoroughbred colt with the rest of his stock. The very best of thinking — the counterpart to which in real life is the sight of a perfectly disciplined, graceful, swift-running horse — begins with the stock, the whole stock, the good and the bad. That is why the regenerate man lets his blooded colt commingle with the rest. He knows the mean and the mediocre can only be counteracted by the influence of the exalted and the best. Swift and slow, bad and good, real and ideal: all of these distinctions are owing to man's natural-supernaturalism, the fact that he keeps the thoroughbred colt with the rest of the stock.

When man speaks or thinks, he leaves his blood behind. Rather, he *releases* his 'blooded colt' — the blood-ties are not to be cancelled as raised to a new level: prophetic rather than determinative. Speaking and thinking are hurdles in the race: particular leaps of self-definition. *Preparation* and *waiting* ripen finally into *action*. In between the waiting and the action is identity, the 'knowing-when.' In human life isn't the 'knowing-when' the knowing of just about everything?

And isn't the 'Blooded Colt' our *true* covenant — the transforming mutuality between biology and biography — without which conceptual saddle we too soon forget how to ride?

X. The Living Being

My grandmother Clara died on February 4, 1979. A year and a half after Nana's passing, my mother died. My father, Paul Johnston, died in the early morning hours of December 8, 1992, at age 84. Within the year, in October, 1993, my oldest brother Tom entered his office, said hello to his partner, sat down at his desk in the adjoining room, and collapsed of a heart attack. In wondering where these people, with all their memories and intentions, have gone, I ask a question as old (or as young) as humanity itself. Indeed, this question hovers "at the edge of history" — both inside history as we know it and outside of it as well.

History is a field of human intentions, deeds, acts. We need to look a little more closely at this field of human intention: for upon it hangs, as if by a silver thread, the concept of the Living Being.

By studying the realm of human intention, we also will try to characterize the nature of a moral act. A moral act has to have something of continuity as well as discontinuity. There has to be a certain freedom, in the sense that it is performed without immediate result and it cannot be an exact repetition of something in the past. A moral act adds something; it brings in something new. On the other hand, this newness cannot be one of mere novelty, which is a kind of 'mechanical' addition. When this happens there cannot be continuity.

Let us look at some of the human acts and intentions mentioned in this book:

(1) Jefferson's "Expurgated Bible": Jefferson's intention to bring Biblical understanding in accordance with reason.

(2) John Hartwell Cocke's emancipation project.

(3) The emancipation project of Frances Wright.

(4) Paul Johnston's support of the civil rights movement.

(5) Martin Luther King's leadership of the civil rights movement.

(6) Clara Johnston's recovery of Bremo

(7) Louisa Cocke's struggle with obedience.

At about the time that General Cocke was engaged in the building of Bremo, Jefferson was laboring to purge the Bible of supernaturalism — attempting to bring the Bible into conformity with rationalism.

Rationalism assumes the relationship of all and all, but it is mainly interested in isolable facts and relations in order to control and direct them. Rationalistic thinking elevates the principle of control to supreme importance, only returning to the relational mode to check or verify its finding. The truth is not in the relation. Rather, the relation itself makes possible the truth, which is viewed as a kind of constructive tool. Thus the old theory of truth — that it "instructs"- is displaced. We no longer seek in knowledge an instructive content to which we may aspire, and which, in aspiring to attain it, encourages us to subordinate and unify our impulses. It is not only that, in a rational age, there has been a "knowledge explosion." There has been. But more than a "knowledge explosion" there has been a change of allegiance. The old ideal of the unification of the soul — integration — ceased to be compelling, if even meaningful. And even when it did not cease to be altogether meaningful, its import was considered to be purely 'psychological' or 'religious' — that is, private. The integration of knowledge as it pertained to public, shared, historical life — this is an ideal that began to fade even long before this.

We modern people, therefore, have inherited a plurality of impulses but not the unifying glass to look at them. The division of head and heart seems most persistent in the history of the rational age — as if it began with the fission that finally exploded in 1945. But there is a more general division between *intellectual* and *material*. We are obviously materially related to the world, a fact verified through common sense and scientific experiment. But our intellectual strivings tend to become "olympian" — more and more complex because there is more and more in the world to incorporate from this lofty intellectual perspective. But how to look where we are going? Intellectual — which is to say, modern — man is somehow cut off at the feet. He is always looking down, always looking for where his feet might actually be touching the ground. Hence there is, with intellectualism, the tendency to simplify and reduce — the intellect's attempt to get to the ground of things. Reductionism and intellectualism go together.

Jefferson's attempts at rewriting the Bible were reductionistic — extremely so. But there is a better way to bring Biblical revelation in accordance with reason. Not through subtraction of parts of the Bible, but through harnessing the powers of what I call the *blooded colt* — a voluntary holding-back, a waiting, and a recognition, on the part of the individual concerned, of what he understands with what he is not yet able to understand. This voluntary act of waiting or active patience is the opposite of *spiritual passivity*. Jefferson presents himself to us as an intellectually superior, though spiritually passive, individual. His "Expurgated Bible" is a monument to spiritual passivity.

This voluntary self-restraint, awareness and acceptance of the limits of one's particular perspective, can have a particular result. The effort to understand something may be touched with reticence. It is not the object itself which stands there, waiting to be stripped and shorn to what it "really is." Rather, I must bring something to it — new objects, settings, a change of scenery or script. I need to see it in many lights. I must help supply the changing light with which to behold this object.

With this thought we approach the nature of a moral deed. A moral deed *adds* rather than subtracts. It brings something *more* to the object than is immediately there, for the sake of doing justice to it – for the sake of *fulfilling* it.

In Christian terms, this initiative is achieved through witnessing in the life, death and resurrection of Jesus Christ — open and available to all who want to participate in it. But paradoxically its very openness helped to bring about the very problem that Christianity has had difficulty in resolving. This was the *imitatio christi* — the "Imitation of Christ." Imitation precedes initiative or initiation — both in human development as well as Christian history. *Imitatio* is in a race with perfection — with the impossibility of perfection. It can have a dampening effect upon initiative, the self-assurance and trust which underlies the expression of will in moral action. Christianity, rightly or wrongly, has sometimes been blamed for undermining these qualities of self-assurance and trust.

We see this problem in Louisa Cocke's struggles with "perfect obedience." Louisa was struggling with the contradictions of an *imitatio* Christianity, while her spouse seems to be moving towards an *initiatory* Christianity. As marital problems go, this one has some claim to possess more than psychological-subjective elements. There is a historical dimension in it as well.

The imaginary conversation between Mr. Cocke and Mr. Jefferson in Chapter Two was an effort to describe one aspect of a modern initiation experience. Through his first wife General Cocke received assurance of the truths of Christian revelation. The General reached another stage of inward assurance in his "conversation" with Jefferson. The conversation provided him with another confirmation of his own path — which was, precisely, a *path*, not a collapse to the dictates of a spiritually passive reason. Gen. Cocke's respect for Mr. Jefferson, genuine as far as it went, did not entail on his part any desire to be like him.

In general, an initiation experience must comprise two parts — the literal or metaphoric "tap on the shoulder" from the male and the female. Male and female are the two streams of our biological heritage. They become transformed in the *biographical* heritage into principles of likeness and difference, union and opposition, common heritage and individual path. The male tap on the shoulder can usher in the oppositional and differing element, or the unifying and common one; likewise with the female. The message is not in the gender of the person doing the tapping but that the principle of complementarity must be accounted for in this twofold way.[1]

Contrast the slave emancipation experiments of Frances Wright and John Hartwell Cocke. To Frances Wright, the evil of slavery existed on the same continuum with marriage and religion. By subtracting these, she thought, she could help work toward the abolition of slavery. But subtraction, in social terms, is never a purely mathematical operation. The French revolutionaries thought that by subtracting the aristocracy you could arrive at "liberty, equality, fraternity." The Communists wanted to subtract the capitalists to arrive at social justice. The pro-choice people think that by subtracting the fetus (abortion) you can serve women's liberation.

There is, indeed, a modern pornography of subtraction: the tireless effort to simplify and reduce, reduce, reduce. Hardly a "clean slate" — for it has exacted a huge toll in the shedding of innocent blood.

Cocke's emancipation program reveals a very different dynamic. Cocke believed that slavery could be overcome only by *adding to it*: religious instruction, education and training, a practical emancipation program. This is what I call the dynamic of the moral act. It is true that both Frances Wright and General Cocke grounded their experiments on a pragmatic, business-like foundation. But here the resemblance ends. Mere pragmatism is not enough. General Cocke's experiment took account of the "changing light" — that is, the spiritual dimension. His efforts had to do with helping the slaves achieve mastery first over themselves — a necessary precondition for the acquisition of that "spiritual power" essential to historical consciousness.

Thus, a moral deed is more than an operation of mechanical addition. Rather, it represents a kind of *metaphoric addition*: i.e., the transfer of spiritual quality. Spiritual quality has no 'weight.'[2] Purely mechanical addition, on the other hand, overloads. Contrast the early history of the civil rights movement — with its "metaphoric addition" of the idea of history as a Living Being — with its later manifestation in quota-thinking and affirmative action, i.e., "mechanical" addition.

These elements also show up again in Frances Wright and her family line. Frances' daughter resisted her mother's "subtractive mentality," and in her son, Kenneth Guthrie, this tendency became fully conscious, for his writings have

---

[1] In Martin Luther King's case, the unifying element seems to have been supplied by his father. See quote following.

[2] It is the addition which 'lightens' – the spiritual dynamic is completely the reverse of the material, where anything added only *increases* the weight -- when a man "may free himself from certain burdens of the past that weighed upon him, when he can find them, face them and integrate them in his consciousness." Note, p. 343, in John Lukacs, *Historical Consciousness,* 1968.

to do with 'adding' the Hierarchies, the Spiritual Beings. Here indeed is "metaphoric addition" on a large scale!

Let us look at Paul Johnston's support of the civil rights movement. My father attained moral act and initiative, but it was at a cost. He was not really able to integrate his acts into his covenant of generations. He was never at home with his heritage; he was at odds with his family and with his forebears. The sadness that afflicted his latter years was a testament to this feeling. He had run the race of the thoroughbred, he had done the moral deed, but the family honor, at least with respect to his own role in it, was still in question.

Like his friend Virginia Durr, Paul Johnston moved from the covenant of generations to the covenant of liberalism. But whereas Virginia Durr could continue to relate to the Code of Southern Womanhood, which she believed she had rejected, Paul Johnston's relational side — apart from family — remained unfulfilled. Perhaps in the triad of Harvard, psychoanalysis, and Unitarianism, there was not a sufficient link to his generational covenant, or perhaps these things – signifying rationalism in advanced forms — allowed a too limited communion with imagination. In any case Paul's trajectory took him to Nuremberg — and the void.

My father's achievement of moral act shows how such morality can become impoverished when it is enacted outside the generational covenant which gives it fullness and embodied life. Paul Johnston was suspended between the generational covenant and modern, government-sponsored liberal morality. Paul at least knew something of the sacrifice that goes into moral achievement. But those who came after, the bureaucrats and social justice engineers, knew nothing of it at all. Morality had become the herd mentality of the modern bureaucratic state, the rationalist dream of a world in which no one should suffer.

The covenant is a context, a particular workable thread in all-that-is — race, folk, family, tradition, or line of inheritance — in which a person's deeds can unfold and in which they have meaning. Contrast my father's position with regard to his family covenant to that of Martin Luther King. In a sober and far-reaching self-assessment, King said of himself: "In the quiet recesses of my heart, I am fundamentally a clergyman, a Baptist preacher. This is my being and my heritage for I am also the son of a Baptist preacher, the grandson of a Baptist preacher and the great grandson of a Baptist preacher."[3] Martin Luther King *was* at home with his generational covenant. The fullness of his leadership in the early days of the civil rights movement, like the fullness and power of his voice, attested to a man at home with his heritage.

My grandmother also felt herself very much within the generational context. Her desire to purchase Bremo, arising in her youth, was fulfilled some thirty years later, on October 12, 1926, when she and Forney bought it. Clara and Forney were able to draw to some extent upon the powers of the *blooded*

---

[3] Eugene Genovese, "The Theology of Martin Luther King," *The Southern Front,* Missouri, 1995, p. 171.

colt — an image for that which in human beings makes possible the expression of the will. What is conceived as desire and intention is later able to manifest as deed and act. But theirs was an essentially *covenantal* rather than *moral* deed – 'covenantal' in the sense of wanting to extend the family context for future generations. This family context, or 'promise of generations,' acted as a strong undercurrent in lives of my grandparents.

My father had the morality of the colt without the honor; his parents had gained the honor without the moral deed. Thus there was, in my family line, something that led to a sense of vexation and incompleteness; of things not quite achieving their appointed goals; of opportunities not so much missed as misinterpreted.

I want to explore this feeling of vexed incompleteness and unfulfillment. Indeed, this feeling is fundamental to our historical experience. If we were solely creatures of the moment, history could have no interest for us. Nor would the colt stir in our blood with aspirations of achievement and honor. The inspiration for a moral deed arises in the *relational* mind — from having a sense of history, or rather, a sense of what history, at that moment, needs. To be relational is to be in partnership with circumstances; it is to seek the permission of circumstances in which to act. This is why, in General Cocke's words, the blooded colt is kept with the rest of the stock. The blooded colt is a vivid image for the *relational* mind. This mind, always in quest of circumstances with which to be "in relation," is not alone, does not exist in and for itself; it belongs with its historical conditions, opportunities, limitations, circumstances. It is with the rest of the stock.

But we are not just "relational" beings. In the very act of perceiving our relations with things, we perceive our separation from them. In this we are thrust into rationality, which shows us both our connection and our abandonment: "And the eyes of both of them were opened, and they knew that they were naked." (Gen.3:7)

History as the Living Being gives us the dynamic tension between the relational and the rational. Our situation today, however, has become critical. Modern man perceives his situation overwhelmingly in rational terms and this rationalism now infects all his ties to life — nature, religion, family, culture, nation, politics, government. Indeed it is not easy to maintain relational ties in a rationalistic age. Those who defend the public expression of such ties, such as the relational bonds of religion, are dismissed as conservatives.[4]

In this regard, another aspect of General Cocke's characterization of the blooded colt is worth pondering. He says that the regenerate man does not

---

[4] Many modern or postmodern doctrines, it could be argued, are anti-rational – although I think that modern anti-rationalism is but a revolt from rationalism, a panic rationalism, not a true arrival to a new relationalism. And it could also be argued that modern conservatives defend relational ties in very 'rationalistic' ways. But what is important is to develop a feeling for 'rational' and 'relational' — and how impervious we seem to think the latter is to endless dismantlement. For example, I read in the *Birmingham News*, that school Bible classes, offered in Dayton, Tennessee, for 51 years, are being suspended because "they violate the constitutional separation

send prayers up to God that his blooded colt will be a distinguished performer on the Turf.

I interpret this to mean that despite the divisions of life in an age of rationalism, the relational mind does not seek to make its cause God's cause. The relationship with God is one among a number of relations, and perhaps it is chief among these. But the God-relation is in the relation, not in "God." To focus one's exclusive attention upon "God" would be to diminish the others, to "de-covenant" or "de-contextualize" oneself from the circumstances. It would be, in a manner, to slight the circumstances – no longer to incline one's ear to them, no longer to be receptive to them. It can lead to fanaticism – which, in Louis de Bonald's definition, is "believing that God perpetually acts without means, like a prince who, relying on God for the care of his defense by a supernatural operation, neglects to levy troops."[5]

The relational mind is in partnership with circumstances. It seeks the permission of circumstances in which to act. In the moment of action — perhaps only in that moment — it is possible to sense the presence of God. This is the moment of "Identity" as moral will. Identity is formed by relations, but it defines itself by its acts. And the general mode for understanding such acts is the concept of honor.

Honor is how relational thinking defends its own particular and limited perspective against the greater abstract and isolating tendency of rationalism. The decision of honor is the agreement to grant full "is-ness"— that is, full being— to a situation that has been compromised by thinking and perceiving. *All* human acts are compromised by thinking and perception — and by much else as well — fear, envy, greed, partisanship, violence, and wrong, to name a few.

This is the *historical* world in which we must act, and in which we make our compact with honor. This compact goes to the depths of our historical life. Honor does not gloss over the compromises of history. It merely tries to rescue the *promise* from the com*promise,* and says: Yes, let us look at that too.

---

of church and state." (Feb. 9, 2002) We misrepresent historical continuity as a threat to our own sufficiency, our autonomy. Thus we imagine to experience autonomy involves committing some act of destruction upon the past or upon historical continuity. It is the antithesis of stewardship. History is "needy": it needs our integration; it calls for acts of reclamation and restoration.

[5] F. Roger Devlin, "Louis de Bonald: Neglected Antimodern," *The Occidental Quarterly*, vol 10, no 2, Summer, 2010.

Epilogue: Intimacy of Fact

The incredible intimacy of fact: if it did not happen, it could not be believed. History yields to us this sense of wonder, that things happen when, how, as, they do; that people appear in unique and unrepeatable circumstances, that they are particular and yet have thoughts that can transcend particularity; that every event, no matter how minute, presupposes the existence of the whole universe; and every event, from the minute, mute and anonymous to the grandiose, loudly-spoken and much-remembered, changes the configuration of the whole; that everything that was or will be, *is*. Water, rock, fire, air: what is history? Not a *natural* element, certainly; nor an *unnatural* one: yet in some deeper sense involved with *Nature* . . .

Maybe the gift of a Southern heritage, of the "Southern conservative tradition," is to raise up this cloak against immediacy, to counter *Gaia* with *Sophia*. For the radical environmentalists conceive of Earth as the Living Being, but their conceptions leave no room for human beings. They exile humanity from the lap of *Gaia*. Some believe the earth would be better without human beings; they would subtract Man altogether. But life on earth without human history can give no framework for the moral; there can be no means of judging the good that human beings do, as well as the evil. The sparks of human deeds can lead to the great conflagrations of history, or they can die away into ashes — in history the *intimacy of fact* derives from *human warmth*.

Perhaps, as the environmentalists warn, the Earth is getting hotter. There is disagreement. But perhaps, as no one to my knowledge has yet warned, history is growing colder. The danger of new glaciation is not from nature but from history.

We have also to acknowledge that moral acts (the 'new' that allows history to continue) encompass a dimension of *power*. It is power in harness, it is power contained, it is spiritual power: nevertheless, it is there and it is real power.

Spiritual power awaits at the threshold of man's historical consciousness. This is the *intimate fact* that the modern world ignores at its peril.

Maybe I have — as the attentive reader may already have noticed — blundered into a contradiction. This contradiction has to do with a distinction made earlier, between *inheriting the earth* and *gaining power*. This was a distinction touched upon by Martin Luther King and Stokeley Carmichael in their discussions relating to black identity. In the course of that discussion Dr. King disagreed with Carmichael's belief that "we must get power at any cost." Dr. King favored a 'programmatic' approach, determination and creative endeavor. Yet I acknowledge that the accession of *spiritual power* is the prerequisite for historical consciousness. Do I thus, in this backhanded way, pass the torch to Stokeley Carmichael? How can I distinguish that *spiritual power* from the kind of power that Stokeley Carmichael was talking about?

By keeping to the narrow band of human warmth, of historical life, we notice that power always involves the question of *means*. Whatever "spiritual power" may be, it involves a relationship between spirit and matter: that when the power is available to achieve something, the means will be found to achieve it. This relationship is more than a matter of faith. Without it history could not be. We are bidden to acknowledge that power cannot be divorced from the question of means — that, in fact, power must consist of finding the means . . . of harnessing the *blooded colt*, who is ready to be led out of the stable into the race.

Postscript to "Stewards of History"

Slavery ended in the United States a few short years after oil was discovered in Pennsylvania. The substitution of fossil fuel for human labor would have ended the slave system sooner or later in any case. But as we stand facing the future of what seems to be the inevitable decline of the oil era, it is sobering to recall the struggle over slavery and what it cost this country. For we have our "energy slaves" in the form of the invisible work performed by oil, gas, and coal. As these storehouses of energy become depleted over the next decades, we will need to think about stewardship in a more fundamental way than ever before. Not all of American history has been characterized by the "get rich quick" mentality. There have been, and are, good stewards here. But we need to find them, and we need to appreciate them. And above all we need to think about what makes good stewardship possible.

This book has been an attempt to explore the foundations of good stewardship: honor, patrimony, the moral deed, the covenant, the 'blooded colt' as metaphor for the will that achieves action. It has been an attempt to forge a new vocabulary for understanding history and for what allows history to continue.

I am a baby boomer. In the more than fifty years that have passed since the ending of World War II, I have witnessed the automobilization of America. Cars – the presence, their needs, their dominance – have overtaken every expanse, every corner, of America. Russell Kirk once called the automobile the "American guillotine," and I have seen nothing in my lifetime to dispute this judgment.[1] Automotive litter has replicated everywhere — a Trail of Tears comprised of gas stations, strip and shopping malls, fast-food joints, parking lots, and office "parks" snaking, worming, and winding out of every American city, town, and suburb, every mountain, valley and dale. *Sunt*

---

[1] His words: "a mechanical Jacobin, overthrowing dominations and powers, breaking the cake of custom, running over oldfangled manners and morals, making the very air difficult to breathe."

*lacrimae rerum*² — while the *civitas* itself stood empty, gaping, and abandoned.³ What reason to go to the city, which in the American twist to an old story, had become the "urban jungle"?

Automotive, automatic, autistic. Barbarism is the lack of relation or relatedness, the reduction into disparate elements, dispersion, isolation, incommunicability. This is what Ortega y Gasset termed the "hermetism" of the mass-mind, in his famous, though misleadingly titled, book, *The Revolt of the Masses*. Ortega talked about the tremendous surge in the European populations from the nineteenth century and what this meant in terms of acculturation. The educational and spiritual resources of society were unable to keep pace with the population explosion that modern science and hygiene made possible. Quantity and technics became the watchword – not quality and striving for something higher. There were no "betters" to imitate. For better or worse the age of the common man had dawned. But what became of excellence and the striving for something higher? The "mass," in Ortegan terms, is not a class of persons, but refers to an attitude of self-satisfaction which has permeated modernity.⁴ For example, the idea of "self-esteem" in modern education has become important in its own right, overwhelming even the fact of disciplined accomplishment to which it once referred.

To Ortega, the "revolt of the masses" meant a revolt from standards. John Lukacs thought that Ortega was mistaken in one important respect. Society as we know it has not really collapsed, as Ortega thought that it might when the "barbarians" took over. The "barbarians" *have* taken over — but they are not lacking in technical skills. John Lukacs wrote: "We know something that people in the beginning of the twentieth century could not even imagine: that the advance of technology and barbarism are no longer irreconcilable."⁵

Christopher Lasch also made a passing allusion to Ortega's book in his *Revolt of the Elites,* which explored the differences between aristocratic and meritocratic societies. To be born into an aristocratic setting takes no talent of one's own. It is a fortunate, but arbitrary, turn of nature — and one which, for that reason, comes with a sense of obligation.⁶ In a meritocracy, on the other

---

² *"Sunt lacrimae rerum et mentem mortalia tangunt."* Always in life are there tears being shed for things, and human suffering ever touches the heart. Virgil, *The Aeneid* I, I, 462.

³ "American architecture is, as a rule, conventional, bland, and dull." Sarah Williams Goldhagen, "Architecture: Boring Buildings," *The American Prospect,* vol.12, no. 22, Dec.17, 2001. Ms. Goldhagen, bracingly, calls for "a nationally accessible architecture curriculum for secondary schools" as a first step in educating Americans to the crying need for a better built environment.

⁴ For such people, ideas are little more than "appetites in words." This is a revealing phrase that shows to what extent we moderns are ruled by our stomachs. It is certainly an inversion of the traditional concept of an idea, that is, contemplation, i.e., the ability to 'behold' or 'see,' implying the refusal to consume.

⁵ John Lukacs, *The End of the Twentieth Century and the End of the Modern Age,* 1993, p. 288.

⁶ The sense of honor is closely related to this. Honor is destroyed by all forms of compulsion. It can live only between a fortune randomly given and an obligation freely offered. Everything conspires against the feeling of self-sufficiency.

hand, people feel they have achieved everything on their own efforts, and are therefore less apt to feel obliged to those less fortunate.

For centuries the butt of many a joke was the first-born son of the aristocracy who was born to the inheritance but refused its obligations, and so relapsed into serious wastrel-hood and profligacy. But all of us now are like firstborn profligates. No aristocracy on earth has ever produced a wastrel like Hydrocarbon Man.

The era of hydrocarbon may prove short. Every 24 hours the global economy burns 73 million barrels of oil.[7] Walter Youngquist says that we are now close to having consumed half of the world's endowment of petroleum. [8] The Oxford-educated petroleum geologist Colin Campbell writes that "about 90% of the world's oil endowment lies in just 30 major petroleum systems —" and these fields are aging.[9] Matthew Simmons, the late Director of Simmons Company International, emphasized this as well: "There are some grim facts that suggest many of the world's existing oil and gas basins are getting quite long in the tooth," he wrote. [10]

Let us, for purposes of hypothesis, take the worst-case scenario. Let us suppose that in the first decade of the twenty-first century, oil fields all over the world suddenly begin to run dry. Let us further suppose that this event has nothing to do with politics, prices, recession, or the market. It is happening because *the oil is simply not there in the ground.* Aside from the economic collapse and widespread famines [11] this event would cause, what would be the result?

We are apt to forget that capitalism, an economic system that has generated great wealth and prosperity, is a word formed from the Latin *capitalis,* head or principal part. *Capital,* in a 1630 definition of the word, is 'accumulated wealth employed reproductively,' and *capitalism* is a system that harnesses and reinvests the wealth accrued by human ingenuity and intelligence.

It is not only that, in the hypothetical collapse of the oil energy system, everyone would realize how much the success of capitalism depended upon the petroleum resources. Most reasonable people already know this. I think the deeper realization would be the question of what had happened to human in-

---

[7] The current figure (2004) is about 78 million barrels daily.

[8] Walter Youngquist, "Spending Our Great Inheritance – Then What?" *Geotimes,* July 1998. Apparently, both oil pessimists and optimists agree that "about half" of the world's reserves have been used up.

[9] Colin J. Campbell, "The Imminent Peak of World Oil Production: Presentation to the House of Commons All-Party Committee, " July 7, 1999.

[10] Matthew Simmons, "Our Energy Crisis: Is it Real? How Does It Get Resolved?" Conoco Senior Management Retreat, March 11, 2001.

[11] Oil is critical in modern agriculture. Bartlett, 1978: "Modern agriculture is the use of land to convert petroleum into food." Pimentel, 1998: "If the fertilizers were withdrawn corn yields, for example, would drop from 130 bushels per acre to about 30 bushels." This is assuming the use of legumes for nitrogen. Without legumes, the yield would be about 16 bushels an acre – a normal harvest in the developing world. From Walter Youngquist, "The Post-Petroleum Paradigm," *Population and Environment: A Journal of Interdisciplinary Studies,* vol 20, no. 4, March 1999.

telligence in the oil-consuming era. How could such fabulous technological power and ingenuity coexist with this apparent abysmal failure of foresight? With such a massive failure to plan for the exhaustion of resources, could the economic system that generated a catastrophe of such proportions have been termed 'capitalist' — that is, intelligence-based — in any true sense?

Here again we meet with what could be called the spiritual problem of modernity: the failure of vision and stewardship. "Petroleum is black magic, the lifeblood of our civilization." [12] The use of the term "black magic" is very telling. It conjures up, not capitalism, but *capitulation* to temptation. On the day the oil ran out, millions of cold and hungry human beings suddenly found themselves *recapitulating* an old, old story that the age of cheap oil had enabled them to forget. Maybe it's as old as the Garden of Eden, which expressed the fundamental notion of stewardship in Genesis 2:15: "And the Lord God took the man, and put him into the garden of Eden to dress it and to keep it."

The energy paradigm is basic to the notion of stewardship: we have to work in order to live; you can't get something for nothing; in this world "infinity" is not a possibility; there are always limits. But the Biblical notion of stewardship has mostly failed to win the hearts and minds of the modern environmentalist movement. The main objection environmentalists made was to an earlier passage in the Creation story, the first creation of man as male-female: "And God blessed them, and God said unto them, Be fruitful and multiply, and replenish the earth, and subdue it: and have dominion over the fish of the sea, and over the fowl of the air, and over every living thing that moveth upon the earth." (Gen. 1:28)

Few make the point that this blessing was delivered to the "unfissioned" or undivided human being who originally existed as the unity of male and female, that is to say, *an integrated whole, sinless*, and *unfallen*. Perhaps the gloss was theologically too abstruse even for those who would defend Genesis, not to mention those who objected to it. Only the sinless human being was to be entrusted by God with "dominion." It could not be presumed that this entrustment would persist after the Fall into Sin had changed the face of mankind and of nature. Such a presumption would indeed be the height of arrogance. It is this presumption, not dominion as such, which is at the root of much that environmentalists rightly object to. As Ortega y Gasset perceived so clearly, modernity has an all but visceral resentment of anything having to do with "dominion" — hierarchy, authority, standards.

But the concept of stewardship stands or falls on the notion of dominion. This is why we need to clarify and understand the concept of dominion, and why it is intellectually dishonest to pretend to wish it away.[13]

---

[12] Randy Udall, *Home Power Magazine*, Feb. 9, 2001 (#81 Bonus Article on http://www.homepower.com/bonus.htm)

[13] Cf. "The deepest cause of the present devastation is found in a mode of consciousness that has established a radical discontinuity between the human and other modes of being and the bestowal of all rights on the humans." Thomas Berry, *The Great Work: Our Way into the Future*, Bell Tower,

A steward is someone who has power or dominion over something, and whose exercise of dominion is beneficial, far-sighted, and life-enhancing. Modern humanity's dominion over nature has proven to be malignant, short-sighted and death-dealing, subversive of both nature and society. The answer is not in an increase of "rights" for non-human living forms but to modify the language of rights, in fact to subordinate it altogether to the language of obligations. "Rights" no longer mean much in a world whose ecology is increasingly threatened and being rendered unstable or infertile.

Stewardship hinges on what view we take towards humanity in the ecology of life. If humanity is just an "evolved ape" the question has no meaning. In the evolutionary scenario there is no reason whatsoever for us to become good stewards because there is no way that an animal, even an advanced one, can become a steward of creation. An animal's niche is "given." The human being's niche is partially given, in a biological sense. But in a deeper sense a human being's niche is history. Man must form his niche. He must learn how to steward himself into being through the "practice" or "industry" of history. I have talked about the values of good stewardship of history in this book – attempting to forge a new vocabulary for the patrimonial values involving honor, gratitude and the sense of obligation. Finding and reawakening this new vocabulary is an urgent task of our time.

History is the mediating term between stewardship and the question of humanity's role in the world. But the ultimate question remains: what is the need for human beings in the universe? What do we supply that nothing else does? What is the purpose and value of our life?

I believe it has something to do with the consciousness of mutuality. Here is a beginning for a metaphysical basis of stewardship, which begins with the acknowledgement of mutuality and of mutual need. Achieving clarity at this level is perhaps the highest spiritual knowledge possible for members of our kind. It means appreciating *all of life*, no less than the life we were given in history.

New York, p. 4. But "rights-talk" is what got us into this predicament; it is not the way of working ourselves out of it.

Appendix One: A Note on Thomas Jefferson

Stewards of History is not a book about Thomas Jefferson. It is a book about history in a very particular and biographical sense, about how certain individuals in one family responded to the great issues of their time. This is a book about learning how to "care for" or be a steward to history, as illustrated in the lives of particular individuals. And in this book, which is about the stewardship of history, Thomas Jefferson does not have the starring role. Perhaps the quality of stewardship or of one's response to history has little to do with one's own mark on the times. "Celebrity" may indeed be a paradox of history – something like one of those illusory visions of an oasis in the desert. [1]

This is not to deny that the Jeffersonian ideal contains elements which are noble, uplifting, and inspiring. The Age of Reason, of which Jefferson was such an enthusiast, must have provided a very favorable climate for thinking and educated people. As John Adams, Jefferson's older contemporary, once noted, the Enlightenment was a period when the arts and sciences useful to man were improved, greatly ameliorating the human condition. And yet, how often has it happened in history, that the Goddess Reason turns into a tyrant?

How else are we to explain Jefferson's enthusiasm for the Jacobin Terror raging in France? For Jefferson, almost than any other American, discredited the idea of an aristocracy. Are all men created equal? This sentence, famous in the Declaration of Independence, made the term "aristocracy" odious in the United States.

Yet this was not fated. The slaughter of aristocracy in America did not come about through the guillotine. It came through the seemingly harmless

---

[1] George Eliot dealt with this paradox in the closing lines of *Middlemarch*: "..that things are not so ill with you and me as they might have been, is owing to the number who lived faithfully a hidden life, and rest in unvisited tombs."

passageway of words, penned by that poet and intellectual, Thomas Jefferson. And remember, it was Jefferson's own kinsman – the inimitable John Randolph of Roanoke, who once declared: "I am an aristocrat. I love liberty, I hate equality." There was no love lost between those two. Perhaps John Randolph foresaw the rivers of blood that would come gushing under the banner of egalitarian idealism. It was another conservative a century and a half later, Georges Bernanos, who saw what perfect equality would mean. "From every victory for equality, each citizen could derive some advantages and personal satisfaction, but the real profit went only to the state. To reduce everything to one common denominator makes dictatorships' problems enormously easier to solve. Totalitarian regimes are the most egalitarian of all: total equality is total slavery!"

But surely – I hear my reader protest – surely the American ideal is about equality?

That so many believe that equality is the ideal of the American founding is a tribute to the power of Jefferson's pen. Yet it would not be fair to blame Jefferson for the political troubles of the 20th century, many of which sprang from a confusion between liberty and equality. It is easier to tear down the barriers that prevent equality than it is to preserve the barriers that act as brakes on the excessive accumulation of power. To *break* – that is, to destroy – may be the default position of the human species. But the mark of the civilized human being is to *brake,* to restrain, to impede the natural flow of impulses. For this reason, liberty is much more difficult to achieve than equality. For liberty acknowledges that that which exists, has the right to exist. In this sense liberty is the fundamental act of affirmation, and echoes the divine pronouncement in the Book of Genesis on the creation of the world: *"It is good!"*

Fundamental affirmation is difficult to achieve under the rationalist dispensation. For liberty affirms the integrity of things for their own sake, not for any meaning it wishes to impose upon it. But it is undeniably true that the things that exist may do so in flagrant and evident injustice. For the rational mind this situation is unacceptable, because it seems to the rationalist that his relationship with the world comes about through *thinking* and not because that is the way, in fact, that things happen to be. If things are the way they are because that is the way we think them, then it is no great leap to conceiving that the things themselves can be manipulated, changed, altered more to our liking.

The power of the State is well served by this passional rationalizing faculty. In fact, the more that it happens that the integrity of historic institutions is undermined, the better it serves the centralization of power.

I don't believe this was the American ideal. That ideal was embodied in a Constitution which sought to limit the powers of government by delicately and subtly attempting to balance the competing claims of liberty and equality. This fine art of balance is what is lost in the passion for equality. And because Jefferson communicated a passion for equality without the balance – I hold him accountable. He is not, on this point, a good steward.

But there are other things. There is the Jefferson cutting out the pages of St. John's Gospel that he found too "supernatural" for his thin reason to digest. As Jaroslav Pelikan delicately put it, in his introduction to *The Jefferson Bible* – "It is still a bit overwhelming to contemplate the sangfroid exhibited by the third president of the United States as, razor in hand, he sat editing the Gospels…" *Sangfroid* indeed.

And yet, and yet . . .Jefferson's reputation in recent years has been tarnished by the legend that he had a love affair with his slave, Sally Hemings. I say "legend" – yet many people believe it. Though *why* people believe it — that, alas, is another question. [2] Though it should be clear to the reader by now that I am not a fan of Thomas Jefferson in certain respects, I believe that this legend is nothing more than a modern continuation of the slander in which the legend was born. The historical karma of Thomas Jefferson, then, has been to be associated with what is at best an improbability and at worst, a deep untruth. [3]

General Cocke appeared to have believed in this story about Jefferson. There was a journal entry by Cocke indicating that he thought Jefferson had had such a *liaison*. In an article reviewing Annette Gordon-Reed's book on the Jefferson affair[4] Sean Wilentz mentioned Cocke's "matter-of-fact diary notations" in this regard, indicating that Cocke evidently believed the story to be true. I regret that I no longer have Cocke's note to refer to, although, as I recall, the journal entry was late – possibly 1852. This is some thirty years after the events were supposed to have happened. Although I too initially was willing to give some credence to this story of the slave-mistress affair, later reading and reflection has led me to believe that General Cocke was mistaken. I am therefore in agreement with William G. Hyland, who mentions Cocke in his 2009 book refuting the Sally Hemings sex charge, *In Defense of Thomas Jefferson: The Sally Hemings Sex Scandal*. He says that Cocke recorded in his diary of 1853 that Jefferson was a "notorious" example of white masters cohabiting with slaves. In 1859 he wrote that Jefferson was an "example of the damnable practice of keeping a slave as a substitute for a wife."

---

[2] Jeff Randolph, Thomas Jefferson's grandson, remarked in 1873 that the calumnies against his family were motivated by "pandering to a ferocious hate of the Southern white man." Nothing has changed since then. From William G. Hyland, Jr., *In Defense of Thomas Jefferson: The Sally Hemings Sex Scandal*, St. Martin's, New York, 2009.

[3] William Hyland points out how "sex, slavery and controversy sell" when he shows how the tax receipts of the Monticello Foundation mushroomed since the official DNA testing that presumably found Thomas Jefferson guilty. They grew from $2 million before the controversy to $13 million after the 2006 DNA test. The Monticello Foundation had insisted for years that the Hemings charge was a slander. All of this is a sad footnote to Jefferson's idealistic belief that "truth can stand alone." Truth cannot stand against ideology, which is one component of brute force. One of the ideological components of brute force today is a feminism that operates under the cover of black history. See previous note.

[4] *New Republic*, March 10, 1997.

Hyland discounts Cocke's testimony on the following grounds: it was based on "inadmissible hearsay"; his diary entry was recorded some thirty years after the events; and "by this time he had come a radical abolitionist" (!) He also adds, that in earlier days, "there was evidence that Cocke was jealous of the credit Jefferson received for starting the University [of Virginia], while Cocke received little or no credit." I have written to Mr. Hyland requesting evidence of this last charge, but as of this date I have received no reply.

While I thus reject the idea that Thomas Jefferson fathered children by Sally Hemings, I do think that a true "intimate history" of Thomas Jefferson needs to be written. But the intimate history that needs to be written is not psychological or psycho-historical, nor is it even solely personal. A true "intimate history" must take account of the relationship of a person to his ideas. Especially is this true of Jefferson, who succeeded so well in expressing his ideas. "Odd thought: Jefferson's cool, measured, amazingly lucid prose, likewise impossible to match, has often struck me as being made of levers and weights, like his machine. He can lift an idea higher than anyone."[5] To grasp the implications of an "intimate history" in this sense we need to consider the relation of thinking and the world — between *thoughts* and *things*.

Fawn Brodie remarks that "for Jefferson, the old Trinity was replaced by the new trinity of Newton, Locke, and Bacon" — these men being most active in bringing about the change of consciousness that was a most notable feature of the Enlightenment. It is not only that this 'new trinity' acquired for Jefferson the status of a religious doctrine, and that he would use a religious expression to describe its significance for him. The old Trinity testified to God's intimacy with the world. "For God so loved the world..." says the Gospel of John – Jefferson's banished Gospel. In the old Trinity, *factuality* itself was drawn into the sphere of intimacy. It was the great binding of fact and value, history and myth, literal and symbolical.

What is remarkable about the "new trinity" that Jefferson embraced is that there is no intimacy in it. This consideration of "intimacy" never entered into the preoccupations of the men of the Enlightenment. By that time, the link between things and the knowledge it is possible to have of them is experienced as belonging almost solely to the realm of mechanical operations and forces. Jefferson may well indeed have been able to "lift an idea higher than anyone." But it is not solely a mechanical facility with ideas that Jefferson is to be credited with.

The idea of 'lifting' has a salvational or redemptive aspect. Jefferson, almost more than any other American, and certainly more than any other president, believed in what could be called *salvation through knowledge*. This is an old Christian heresy known as gnosticism. The old Christian gnosis at least had Christ at the center, and carried with it the hope of the redemption of the intellect. But the Jeffersonian gnosis is emptied of all religion – just as all that

---

[5] Max Byrd, *Jefferson, A Novel*, New York, Bantam, 1994, p. 93.

was "supernatural" in the life of Christ was cut out of the Jefferson Bible. It is intellect without spirit.

Jefferson's impulse of rationalism in religion, separation of church and state, and salvation through knowledge, all look very different today from what they were in the 1820's. He had great reserves to draw upon. He could presume the continuity of civilization and of civilized men. We no longer have that luxury. Intellectual freedom begins to resemble self-indulgence when it is later generations who have to pay the debt.

Appendix Two: "But...this was not death, but life..."

The following is a copy of letter from Sallie F. Brent to her brother W.R.C. Cocke at Belmead following the death of their father John Hartwell Cocke at Lower Bremo on July 1, 1866. It summarizes many of the themes in this book and thus may serve as its elegiac conclusion.

Lower Bremo
July 15, 1866

My precious Willie

Your sweet letter of the 25th helped me to shed the first tears after "those first dark days of nothingness," when we sit in tearless silence, wondering at the mysteriousness of our being, and awed into utter silence, when Death comes into our midst – But dear Willie this was not death, but life; for I felt that his spirit had almost fled, while yet his feeble frame lingered among us – It was the most gentle, gradual falling to sleep of the "earthly tabernacle," I had ever imagined. Sleeping day, and night, with the quietness of an infant, and not ill 24 hours, and so rapidly did he pass away that I don't think he was aware of his sufferings on that last day. His countenance beamed as with the light of Heaven after Death; and those calm, brilliant nights and days seem to assure us of his rest. I know it was a pang to you dear Willie not to see him again, but as God willed it otherwise, I can tell you that your last letter to him was one of the few things that sent a thrill of joy through his heart, and made him willing to live a little longer. He thanked God that He had permitted him to live to hear what he had on that day, and prayed that he might be more patient and willing to live than he had been. That letter to you was one of the last he ever attempted to write. His heart yearned over you all, and what seemed

sternness toward those most near and dear to him, was from the excess of his anxiety to see them superior to the common herd, and to see them living above the world and its sordid selfishness. I bless God every year I live, for his training of me, for every thing he in *wisdom* denied me, and for every precept he instilled into me, all of which has been to me a mine of happiness, far beyond any other inheritance he could have left me. May his mantle fall upon some of his descendants, and may we "look upon his like again." I love to think, and try to picture his happiness in Heaven, with all the dear ones, who have gone before, whom he loved and above all in the presence of that Savior whom he served so faithfully on earth. This is all worth living for, dear Willie, "Earth's little while" will soon be over and then his [thus by transcriber; in original probably 'how'] insignificant will the toys and rubbish of this life appear, to which we give so much time, and thought. I hoped you would have come up ere this, but I could not let Peyton go down without a line, and shall still hope to see you soon. We hope to get off early in August to the mountains, and wish some of you could join us. Dr. B. will not consent to go without me, and his health is so precarious, I think it his duty to try and strengthen himself as soon as possible. He sends love to you and all mine to your whole household.
Yours ever truly

S.F.B.

BIBLIOGRAPHY

Bankhead, John H. *Memorial Addresses on the Life and Character of Joseph Forney Johnston*, Washington, D. C., 1915.

Belgion, Montgomery. *Victor's Justice*. Henry Regnery and Company, 1949.

Brodie, Fawn. *Thomas Jefferson: An Intimate History*, New York, 1974.

Butler, Stuart L. "General Cocke in the War of 1812." *Magazine of Albemarle County History*, 2007.

Coyner, Boyd. *John Hartwell Cocke of Bremo: Agriculture and Slavery in the Antebellum South:* Ph.D. Dissertation, University of Virginia, 1961.
—— "John Hartwell Cocke: Southern Original," in *Bulletin of the Fluvanna County Historical Society*, No. 6, June 1968.

DuBois, W.E.B. "The Riddle of the Sphinx," in *The Burden of Race: A Documentary History of Negro-White Relations in America*, ed. Gilbert Osofsky, New York, 1967.

Durr, Virginia. *Outside the Magic Circle*, ed. Hollinger F. Barnard, University of Alabama, 1985.

Eaton, Clement. *Freedom of Thought in the Old South*, Duke University Press, 1940.

Eckhardt, Celia Morris. *Fanny Wright: Rebel in America*, Cambridge, Harvard University Press, 1984.

Elkins, Stanley. *Slavery*, University of Chicago, 1959.

Emerson, O.B. "Frances Wright and Her Nashoba Experiment," *Tennessee Historical Quarterly*, December, 1947.

Eskew, Glenn. "The Alabama Christian Movement for Human Rights and the Birmingham Struggle for Civil Rights, 1956-1963," by Glenn T. Eskew, in *Birmingham, Alabama, 1956-1963: The Black Struggle for Civil Rights,* edited by David J. Garrow, Brooklyn, N.Y., 1989.

Faust, Drew Gilpin. *John Henry Hammond: A Design for Mastery,* Louisiana State, 1982.

Garrow, David J.*Bearing the Cross*: *Martin Luther King, Jr. and the Southern Christian Leadership Conference,* New York, 1988.

Genovese, Eugene. *The Southern Front,* Missouri, 1995.

———*The Southern Tradition: The Achievements and Limitations of an American Conservatism.* Harvard, 1994.

Grizzard, Frank Edgar.*'A Perilous and Grievous Burden' The Dilemma of the Antislavery Slaveholder in Virginia During the Early National Period: A Case Study of General John Hartwell Cocke,* Master's Thesis, University of Virginia, May, 1989.

Hyland, William G. Jr. *In Defense of Thomas Jefferson: The Sally Hemings Sex Scandal.* St. Martin's Press, New York, 2009.

Jefferson, Thomas. *Notes on the State of Virginia,* University of North Carolina Press, 1954.

Lauenstein, Diether. *Biblical Rhythms in Biography*, Floris Books, Edinburgh, 1974.

Lytle, Andrew. "Afterword: A Semi-Centennial," in *Why the South Will Survive,* University of Georgia, 1981.

Lukacs, John. *Historical Consciousness*, New York, 1968; second ed., 1985.

Malone, Dumas. *Jefferson and His Time: The Sage of Monticello,* Boston, 1981.

May, Henry F. *The Enlightenment in America,* Oxford, 1976.

Miller, Randall. *Dear Master: Letters of a Slave Family,* University of Georgia, 1990.

Moore, William Cabell. "John Hartwell Cocke of Bremo," *William and Mary Quarterly Historical Magazine,* July, 1933.

Neuhaus, Richard John. *The Naked Public Square*, Eerdman, 1984.

Nunnelley, William A. *Bull Connor,* University of Alabama, 1991.

Oates, Stephen B. *Let the Trumpet Sound: The Life of Martin Luther King, Jr.* New York, 1982.

Rosenstock-Huessy, Eugene. *The Christian Future,* New York, 1946.

Salmond, John A.*The Conscience of a Lawyer: Clifford J. Durr and American Civil Liberties, 1899-1975*, Tuscaloosa, University of Alabama Press, 1990.

Tucker, St. George. *A Dissertation on Slavery : with a Proposal for the Gradual Abolition of It in the State of Virginia,* Philadelphia, 1796.

Urbach, Jon Leonard. *God and Man in the Life of Louisa Maxwell Holmes Cocke: A Search for Piety and Place in the Old South*, Ph.D. Dissertation, Florida State, 1983.

Warren, Robert Penn. *Who Speaks for the Negro?* New York, 1965.

MANUSCRIPT COLLECTIONS

J.C. Cabell Papers, University of Virginia.

Armistead Gordon Papers, University of Virginia.

J.H.Cocke Papers, Accession 640, University of Virginia.

"Birmingham, Ala. Police Department Surveillance Files, 1947-1980," Accession 1125, Birmingham Public Library.